PROFESSIONAL BUM

Lessons Learned from My Twentysomething Adventures

TONI JEFFREY

Published in Felton, California, By the Author

Library of Congress Control Number: 2024926230.

ISBN 979-8-9918332-0-2 (hardcover)
ISBN 979-8-9918332-1-9 (paperback)
ISBN 979-8-9918332-2-6 (ebook)
ISBN 979-8-9918332-3-3 (audiobook)

Printed in the United States.

First Edition

Book design by Rasel Khondokar

Cover design by Boyd Tveit
(www.tveitcreative.com)

To Michael, Tara, Val, and Robbie

CONTENTS

Welcome To The Jungle

Hi, I'm Toni, and I will be your raconteur. So WTF is a professional bum? Thanks for asking.

When people would inquire about my occupation during my twentysomething travels, I would respond that I was a professional bum. I suppose that job title has once again become applicable because I was forced into an early retirement during the Great Recession of 2008-09. My and my husband's stinking company didn't need us anymore. Well, fine; we don't need you! Not exactly...I first had to cry, panic, and make contingency plans to make our car suitable for serving as a temporary residence.

Thankfully, I and my husband made decent money and were very good about saving. We also didn't buy crap such as $100 app-controlled coffee mugs. Geez, Americans will buy anything.

In sum, I was a professional bum in my early twenties. Now I have been a retired professional bum for 15 years and counting. But don't worry; I am not costing you taxpayers a thing. I even do a lot of volunteer work. Take that!

Before I recount my journeys, I will tell you a bit about me and my motivations to seek out so many weird, wonderful, and sometimes boring places. The Lessons Learned from my adventures--hence, the book's subtitle--will be shared when appropriate.

Because this is my book and I make the rules, I will occasionally incorporate "fast forwards," "fast backwards," and a prequel or two. Not everything entertaining in my life happened in my twenties. Thankfully.

Ultimately, I hope you feel as if you were traveling with me, but lone wolf me is glad you did not. I had places to go, people to meet, and things to see. No time to negotiate with a travel companion.

I'm trying to be mostly fun and deadpan. After all, what does David Sedaris have that I don't have? Oh yeah, fame, fortune, and multiple book tours. But aside from that, what?

If you read one book a year, it should be mine. And if you aren't completely satisfied, read a celebrity's memoir if that's your thing. My book is better than Joe Trohmann's. But you probably don't know who Joe Trohmann is.

PART ONE

Leaving tomorrow. I should start my journal by introducing myself, my benign childhood traumas, and my motivations for hitting the road. That'll intrigue my readers because I'm so interesting. And I'd promised my fellow fast-friend travel companions that I would eventually write a book about my adventures because it would make a great memoir.

—Journal entry, March 26, 1985*

*Not really. I wrote this a couple of weeks ago.

But Enough About Me

I hope and assume you know what a raconteur is. Just in case, the internet defines it as "a person who tells anecdotes in a skillful and amusing way." Yeah, I'm trying to be that person.

Humor me for a few pages. If I run into you at the espresso place, we can gab. I'll be the one in the Tom Petty T-shirt.

No Lessons Learned in this chapter, but we're just getting started.

I Finally Wrote the Book

I traveled across many parts of the US and Europe in 1985 and 1986. While I was traveling, several people told me I should write a book. Why has it taken me so many years to do so?

- I and my husband raised three great kids, all of whom are launched. But kids take a lot of time. My travel experiences sustained me through the years when I was up to my neck in dirty diapers and infant vomit; it was an important support system. Toni, you used to be cool! But at those moments, I had to continue changing diapers and cleaning up vomit. And of course I did; my kids needed me. And trust me, you become immune to diapers and vomit. In fact, poop doesn't smell…until they start eating solid foods.

- In spite of notable exceptions, I've never been too interested in autobiographies or biographies. I tried to read about Bob Dylan, Pete Townshend, and Tom Petty, but none of them held my attention; not even Tom's, which embarrasses me. If none of these amazing artists held my attention, my self-doubts made me question why anyone would be interested in the thoughts of a benign person who has retired in my beautiful mountain town.

- OMG, my kids will find out what I did! Everything I taught them not to do! Upon reflection, however, I have come to realize that I didn't do anything too awful. Sure, I partied too much on occasion, but I didn't break any laws. Okay, I did break one law, but didn't get caught and would prefer not to go into it.

Having answered that so-far-unasked question, my goals are now as follows:

- To compare my previous experiences with present-day reflections. I have now reached the big six-oh, so this is the time to tell my story while I am still moderately cool. I intended to include travel journal excerpts that were witty, but discovered that most consist of recurrent memories of "I just slept on the bus with a stinky bathroom and irritating passengers. I wish that creepy guy would stop hitting on me." I may occasionally supply a journal quote, but most of them are too mundane even for me.

- To throw in fun facts whenever I can. Even though this is technically a memoir, it is not all about me-me-me and how I spent my summer vacations. Do you know how you can use the Scoville scale to avoid eating a chili pepper that can set your mouth on fire? Do you know what a garbage plate is? (Hint: Not what you think it is unless you are from Rochester, New York.) Do you know there was a stage play in which fat Elvis Presley viewed his performances when he was young and svelte? And please don't break my heart and tell me you don't know who Paul Collins is, although you probably don't. Sigh. He deserved much more fame.

- To encourage people of all ages to see the world, whether they be twentysomethings with no family obligations or retirees with too much time on their hands. The world is a great and beautiful place. People are great and beautiful. Almost none of them is dangerous. Not too many are armed with AR-15s.

This is not a dress rehearsal (yes, somebody said that before me). Have a blast, and join with me on memory lane. Perhaps you will learn my lessons before you have to do so firsthand.

One more thing: Get off my lawn. As I said, I am only moderately cool.

A Moderately Complex Kid

I don't want to dwell on my childhood, but I thought I should let you know who I was and who I am. Must a memoir provide a synopsis of childhood trauma? But mine isn't awful, just irritating.

I am the youngest of four, and my parents had a rather dysfunctional relationship. I learned at an early age to tune it out, and did so rather successfully. I never-ever missed a meal, but it certainly was not an idyllic household. It was nice when people just shut up.

Thank God for the person who invented headphones, the precursor to the Bluetooth thing. I didn't need arguing parents when I could listen to Pink Floyd's "Dark Side of the Moon" uninterrupted. This album is the fourth bestselling of all time; listen to it if you haven't already done so. Technically, Michael Jackson's "Thriller" is the bestselling ever, but unfortunately I thought I was too jaded and cool to listen to the youngest member of the Jackson Five. Bad me.

When I started school, I was always the smart kid. At that time, schools didn't know how to handle kids as brilliant as me (LOL). For that reason, they sent me into classrooms with older students because I was just too smart to study with kids my own age. I was a first grader studying reading with fourth graders, a second grader studying with fifth graders. In other words, the weird braniac.

When I reached third grade, I had enough and decided I was done with the awkwardness of studying with sixth graders. My parents, God bless them, didn't know how to handle my prodigious intellect (LOL again) either, so they deferred to the school's judgment…nice way of saying my Dad needed to make a living and my Mom needed to deal with three other kids. Their goals for the four of us were to stay out of jail, go to college, and don't get pregnant. Of course, I was too young to do any of those things at that time.

I continued through school, made friends, and had a couple of crushes on guys that were not too good for me (pattern beginning, sigh). However, I graduated high school and college, emerging not too worse for the wear. I still treasure the photos of my parents grinning like idiots the night we went out to celebrate my college graduation.

Childhood trauma over. Adult trauma…ongoing.

I Don't Fit In

Before I continue, I have to thank Paul Collins for his solo acoustic show in my humble town in 2019, at which he sang my life with his words: "I Don't Fit In." He even talked to me after the show! Even your elders probably don't know who he is, but he was awesome. As a member of the semi-legendary punk band The Nerves, he co-wrote the song "Hanging on the Telephone," which Debbie Harry's band Blondie covered. Your elders probably heard of Blondie; if they didn't, no worries; it was and is a great song. And Paul Collins, you must tour again. No, you're not too old.

What does this memory have to do with my travels? I guess it is that I was equally running away and running to. And knowing that nobody knew the young, braniac me, just the twentysomething me, was pleasant. I like to think twentysomething Toni was more interesting. Maybe.

I don't always feel that I don't fit in. But any time I feel like I do, I have to back off and think, "I'm sorry, I didn't mean that." Why is that?

Aside from my aforementioned trauma of being the smart weirdo, it was partially due to my chaotic childhood living in a pigsty. I would go to friends' (clean) houses with friends' (seemingly) sane parents, and just felt like a weirdo. At the same time, I felt like growing up to have a normal life was somehow a betrayal of my family. I think the self-help profession refers to it as "survivor's guilt."

Happily, I and my husband raised three decent kids, and I'm pretty sure their childhoods were much more pleasant than mine. All of them are doing well now, but you'll have to ask them if they agree with me.

Planning, Schmanning

Easy decision to travel on my own. No overthinking needed. As the selfish person I was and still am to an extent, I had no desire to spend a finite amount of travel time negotiating with another person regarding what time to get up, what to see, where to go. Not to mention sharing a room. Yikes.

Back in the pre-internet dark ages, I had to snail mail self-addressed stamped envelopes (I know, what are those?) to tourist commissions (I know, what are they?) to receive glossy brochures reassuring me their city was a Great Place to Visit. I also had to refer to actual books, such as the late, great "Let's Go" series, in order to locate the frugal lodging deals.

The planning was on. I would eagerly visit my mailbox as my pile of travel brochures grew ever higher. In addition, I secured the entire season's Major League Baseball schedules in order to visit as many ballparks as possible. (Yes, I'm a baseball fan and will devote an entire chapter to my fangirl experiences. Trust me, you'll love it even if you know squat about baseball.)

As I perused my pile on my crappy kitchen table, my dreams of seeing the US and Europe began to coalesce. I imagined seeing the greatest museums, the great historical sites, the greatest tourist attractions. Although I did do that, who knew that my fondest memories would be of the dumb things people said to me, dumb things I said to people, dumb decisions I made that didn't kill me, random encounters that I remember to this day? Travel is weird and wonderful in that respect.

I theoretically planned my trip. Two days here, three days there, make sure I'm in town for the baseball game. But aside from game logistics, it was all for naught.

Instead, I planned my route based on bus and train schedules. "Okay, I can't afford accommodations tonight. Which itinerary would allow me to sleep reasonably undisturbed and arrive at my destination after sunrise?" I failed at that once, and had to cower on a park bench in Virginia for two hours. Thankfully, that only happened once.

I am still pleasantly astonished that I ended up neither kidnapped, raped, nor murdered. Just pestered routinely, but learned to handle and rebuff it.

Robert Burns, a poet you may have heard of, had a reasonably famous line: "The best-laid plans of mice and men often go awry." Who knew he was also a travel advisor?

Inquiring Minds Want to Know

Not sure if every written work has to include FAQs, or if that only apply to websites trying to sell you stuff.

Even though we're just getting started, I'm crossing my fingers that I've intrigued you to the extent that you have questions about my story. If these questions haven't occurred to you yet, hopefully they will at some point. Maybe.

Only three Lessons Learned in this chapter, but they're really important ones.

Why should I read your book?

Because I want to brag? Because Rick Steves doesn't know everything about Europe? Because anonymous TripAdvisor reviewers may not be as well-traveled as they imply? (Booger69, did you really go to Italy or are you sitting on your bed in your parents' basement staying awake with the help of multiple energy drinks?) Sorta, yes, and yes.

Not sitting in a rocking chair yet, but I want to let my family, friends, and readers know that I wasn't always the pandemic-induced slug I have become.

In 1982, I actually jumped on stage during a Tom Petty concert, kissed him, and evaded security, although I had a serious fat lip after I dove off the stage with nobody breaking my fall. I thought the fans would come to my rescue, but no. Ask my friend Matt (who witnessed the encounter although he attended the show with someone else) about it. He still tells that story.

In addition, I and my friend Melody hosted a talk show on public access TV for one season in 1992. (We wanted to be on TV, so we gave them a few bucks and were so there.) One of my coworkers dismissively assumed that we simply invited our friends to be our guests, but that was untrue. We reached out to members of our community engaged in various pursuits: writing books, coaching soccer teams, staging improv comedy, organizing community projects, writing personal ads in search of dates (no Tinder swipe-right or -left back then.) Mel and I truly enjoyed having genuine conversations with genuinely nice people eager to publicize their efforts to our 15 or 20 viewers.

Unfortunately, I've accepted that I will never master the buzzer well enough to be a Jeopardy contestant. In 1999, I appeared on "Win Ben Stein's Money," a Comedy Central game show, and stunk because I couldn't master the gosh-darn buzzer. I promise, I knew the answers, but sigh. You can probably watch my show on some archive online, but it was awful. Please God, don't let any of my readers find my appearance on some obscure game show website.

And I had a letter published in Creem magazine while I was in high school. Trust me, this is impressive.

Where did you go?

Hooray, an easy question.

In our nation, I went to states located on the eastern-ish half of our nation: Alabama, Florida, Georgia, Illinois, Indiana, Kentucky, Louisiana, Maryland, Michigan, Mississippi, Missouri, New Hampshire, New Jersey, New York, Ohio, Pennsylvania, Tennessee, Texas, Virginia. Not in that order. (In case you hadn't noticed, the states are in alphabetical order. That's just who I am.) And I passed through several other states when I returned to the left coast, although out of necessity.

In Europe, I went to Great Britain, Ireland, Italy, Northern Ireland, Spain, and West Germany (its name at the time). I also had a quick stopover in France, which I only vaguely remember.

Okay rich girl, how did you pay for all of this?

Not a rich girl, but I got a few bucks from my family due to a home Dad and his siblings inherited after my grandma passed. I must emphasize that it was a few. Jeff Bezos, Bill Gates, or Laurene Powell Jobs would account for it as a rounding error.

Anyway, I paid for these trips as follows:

- For my first trip, I had a long-distance Bad Boyfriend, one in an unfortunate parade (more about them later in this chapter). I talked to him entirely too much via long distance, which gave me a ridiculous amount of reward credits. Back then, long-distance calls actually cost money, and AT&T had a rewards program that enabled me to obtain a free Greyhound "Ameripass," which entitled me to unlimited bus travel for three months. Someone was probably terminated because I cost Greyhound a lot of money.

Because of the aforementioned bus pass, I decided that I would only rent rooms every third night, sleeping on buses for the other two. Sleeping on buses became a skill I quickly learned. As you can imagine, when I had an actual bed, I would watch bad TV and enjoy an actual bed, complete with blankets and pillows. Oh, the life.

- For my second trip, I used the money I did not spend because of all the gosh-darn nights sleeping on buses during my first trip, as well as the intermittent under-the-table work I did for my employer.

- For my third trip, I had accumulated a rather small amount of "profit sharing" from my employer. It was intended to be a start on an eventual retirement account, but retirement was, like, a thousand years away. Thank God Dad didn't find out I used my profit sharing in such a quixotic manner; he was always adamant about saving for a rainy day, and I have come around over the years in that respect. As I write this, I can distinctly hear the sound of him rolling over in his grave. On the other hand, if I did the prudent thing, I would not have been able to write this book.

What are your favorite things?

Another easy question.

My wonderful family, Tom Petty, baseball, and my status as a practicing Catholic (as I practice, I'm sure I will get better). I will incorporate anecdotes about all four of these throughout.

Obviously, I didn't have my husband and kids during my adventures, but I do use my Lessons Learned to try to be a better wife and Mom, even to this day. At this point, all four of them teach me as much as I hopefully taught them. Well, I don't think I teach my husband; he's a grown man, but maybe? He teaches me stuff too, even yesterday.

Trying to include Tom Petty references without overdoing it. It's odd, but Tom was a bigger part of my life than my parents were. I was 28 when I lost my Dad and 38 when I lost my Mom. But gosh, when I lost Tom in 2017, he had been a part of my life for 40 years. I am allowed to continue missing him, and I do. So much.

Baseball, baseball, baseball. I am hoping I can make ballparks intriguing even if you're not a fan. I will not be debating balls, strikes, or the infield fly rule (WTF?), but rather how the same game can be experienced in different ways depending on the venue.

I am a reasonably good cradle Catholic, which means I have been Catholic since I was baptized at the ripe old age of two months. I honestly enjoy the Catholic rituals, but sometimes I struggle to embrace them. I realize that I don't go to Mass to be entertained, but I love when I exit with an enthusiastic vow to serve our Lord and one another. Some priests are better at inspiration than others. I miss Father Scott!

As I recount my memories and subsequent lessons, be assured that I am not trying to convert you to Catholicism, convince you to love baseball, or make you a rabid Tom Petty fan. On the issue of the latter, though, you gotta listen to the 1997 San Francisco Fillmore residency shows. All twenty of them.

You were a young woman traveling solo. Did you ever get scared?

I honestly was scared on only three occasions. Hitchhiking in Tennessee (is hitchhiking even a thing anymore?); having some menacing person follow me on a street in downtown Orlando after the stores were closed; returning to San Francisco at a godawful hour.

In the many zero-star hotels I stayed in, I simply employed the magic of barricading my door and sheltering in place after dark. And occasionally gabbing with the nocturnal bugs. Yes, I am joking. I never gabbed with bugs…just murdered them.

As my travels progressed, I also got meaner and more aggressive towards men who violated my personal space. I also perfected my "badass walk," which consisted of walking down the street with a don't-even-try-to-mess-with-me attitude. I think I still know how to do that, although it's rarely necessary. I think I will be able to modify it when I reach my rocking chair stage…perhaps a "badass stare." It could happen.

Lesson learned: Badass walk. Launch F-bombs occasionally. Throw punches when warranted. I think I can still do my badass walk, but it's not really necessary living in a small town. And definitely not necessary when I sleep in a comfy bed every night.

What is your fondest memory?

Continue reading! Not sure if I can pick just one, but refer to my last vignette in "Take Me Out to the Ballgame."

What do you regret?

- Not venturing behind the Berlin Wall via the Brandenburg Gate, which was semi-affectionately referred to as Checkpoint Charlie at the time (if you appreciate gallows humor). I really meant to do that, but it was just too cumbersome of a trip. I had a friend that was able to witness the awful condition of East Germany before the Berlin Wall fell in 1991. I'm sure it would have been depressing, but I wish I could have seen it with my own eyes.

- Not visiting the Baseball Hall of Fame in Cooperstown, NY. Again, it was just too hard. I still might make it there before my rapidly approaching rocking chair era. If Barry Bonds is inducted at any point, I will need to bring a giant asterisk to benignly vandalize his plaque.

- Not touring Chicago's Sears Tower--now the Willis Tower-- although I have had many, many chances. Traveling on my own, the trip was too hard when a baseball game was happening at 1:00 (only day games at Wrigley Field back then). Traveling with my family, the line was too long. Traveling with my husband, we were just too tired after an overnight train trip. At least we made it to the top of the John Hancock Tower, which is just as fear-inducing, but in a good way.

- Not getting my kicks on Route 66.

How did your family react to your traveling alone at such a young age?

Short answer, it didn't matter. Longer answer, read on.

During one of my periodic phone calls, Mom told me I'd better stop "gallivanting around" or I'd never want to work again. Um, no. And does anyone know what "gallivanting" means anymore?

Of course, many people worried that I was too stupid to not die. Because I didn't die, I guess I figured out how to take care of myself. Because I knew I needed to eat, I skillfully alternated actual meals with cheap ramen noodles boiled in my portable hot pot.

And because of my Walkman (a ubiquitous personal listening device Back in the Day), I could simply listen to some great music when it became too much.

What was the most exhilarating aspect of your travels?

Hooray, another easy question. I woke up and did not know what would happen each day.

I woke up today and pretty much knew what would happen. Knew I would greet my terrific husband. Knew I would have my usual yummy and horribly nutritious breakfast. Knew I would catch up on good reading that might teach me something. Knew I would sleep in my warm and cozy bed. On the road, not so much.

Virtually every day was a crapshoot. Kinda like when we were raising our three kids, who would puke, argue, and/or require urgent care on any random day. Some days I was forced to deal with a yucky powdered-but-reconstituted egg breakfast at a Greyhound station; others I had an astonishingly cheap sit-down and yummy meal.

Some nights I stayed in a zero-star room that frightened me; others I stayed in an embarrassingly posh place I was somehow able to afford. The latter didn't happen very often, but OMG when it did, sigh.

Some days involved surprisingly fun outings and others extremely stupid ones. Some days included gorgeous weather; others were horribly hot, horribly rainy, or both on the same day. Definitely appreciated sunny California.

Bring on the day! But please, no powdered eggs.

Why do you bother to mention Bad Boyfriends? You broke up with them; isn't that good enough?

Because I hope my young women readers will learn from my mistakes before they make them themselves.

No gory details, especially because my kids will hopefully read this book. Aside from that, you would probably laugh in disbelief and assume I was engaging in literary license if I recounted my parade of bad romantic choices. But no. Back in my teens and twenties, I didn't need no stinking self-esteem.

I really didn't have many dates during my travels. However, I did have a handful, most of which reinforced the pattern of my life. "Who is the biggest loser in this room? That's the guy I want to spend time with." I have dated exactly one guy who was not a loser, and I married him. Somehow I knew it would all work out eventually. And it did…in 1996.

I won't dignify any of my Bad Boyfriends with an actual reference to their names. I wonder how many of them are still alive, but it is too much trouble to locate and dance on their graves.

Okay, I might dance on the grave of one of them if I happened to be in the area, which I probably will not be. However, I doubt his family or friends (if he has any, after the miserable life I assume he ultimately led) would be willing to spend the money for an actual grave. They could probably cremate him and throw the ashes in Giants Stadium to enhance Jimmy Hoffa's purported burial place. Or simply go out to sea and throw his body overboard if that were legal. Talk about a wasted life.

That said, I would probably visit the grave of another nameless one if it didn't require much travel. You never forget your first real love. And I hope his life turned out well.

Lessons (eventually) learned:

- Duh. Never date an adult who doesn't have a valid driver's license.

- A Bad Boyfriend can be equated to a broken clock that's right twice a day. If I traveled to an ultimately cool place the jerk mentioned during our dysfunctional relationship, that didn't mean he was a decent human being.

- The six most dangerous words for a woman: "I think I can change him."

What's up with the cultural references I may or may not understand?

You may or may not notice the numerous cultural (mostly musical) references throughout, but I was compelled to quote artists more talented than I. I love music, but when researching the rules regarding using actual lines from actual songs, I would have to secure licensing rights to include them. I would also have to pay money. Too. Much. Bureaucracy.

Instead, I incorporate cultural references whenever I am clever enough to think of them. Yes, I have included several of Tom Petty's songs, but not enough for anybody to come after me. Because song titles cannot be copyrighted, let's go "Running Down a Dream."

I decided to exercise discretion. I mean, come on. Is there just one female singer on the planet who has decided to copyright the term "bad romance" such that nobody else can use it? Is there one band who has decided "take me to the river" is their exclusive phrase nobody can use without paying them? For that reason, I abide by copyright laws. If you encounter a title that makes only a slight amount of sense, ask the internet and you'll probably see what I am tangentially referring to. I can't afford to be sued, plus court appearances are boring.

Interesting to see which cities inspire the most songs. Of course, San Francisco (somebody left their heart there), New Orleans (you can know what it means to miss it), and of course New York (start spreading the news). But who writes songs about Baltimore? Birmingham? Ohio? And Nebraska, for crissakes? I am astonished and impressed that some have had the talent to write songs about Nebraska. Bruce Springsteen, I'm talking to you.

I enjoyed discovering the songs I didn't already know about. If you ask the internet for songs about your town, I bet you would be surprised.

Did you actually experience all these adventures as a twentysomething or are you cheating?

Good question, although I realize that nobody is likely to ask at this point.

As I begin to describe my footloose and fancy-free time, many of my memories reminded me of other places I have been fortunate enough to experience with my husband, three kids, or all of them. Wondering if one of my three kids will write a book specifying how I have gotten those trips all wrong. Hopefully not, but I haven't. Really.

Full disclosure: I have designated those post-twentysomething vignettes with a fast-forward designation. But gosh, I couldn't leave out the National Civil Rights Museum at the Lorraine Motel, the Sainte-Chapelle, or the Sts. Peter and Paul Basilica for the sake of travel purity. I learned lessons from them as well, and would be selfish to refrain from sharing them.

Or perhaps I just need to add more pages to this book to increase its marketability.

Tell the truth. Did you use AI to write any of this?

In a word, hell no. Oops, that's two words.

PART TWO

Hi Mom and Dad--I'm learning very quickly how to familiarize myself with a new city. That is the biggest challenge because time spent finding my way around could be time spent sightseeing. I've already gotten a lot better at it, though.
People have been very helpful and I have had no real problems.
Once again, DON'T WORRY! I'm doing fine!
Sorry I can't wish you a happy anniversary in person, but I'm thinking of you always.

--Greeting card, April 10, 1985

Let the Wild Rumpus Start

When I started to plan this book, I quickly realized it would be useless and confusing to try to present my travels in chronological order. "So I'm in name-of-town, will sleep on a bus, spend the day in name-of-another-town, and sleep on another bus." Even I'm bored by that, and I lived it.

Because my trip was so chaotic and random, let's make it entertaining instead, and group experiences based on themes: churches, baseball, great places, awful places, under-the-table working gigs, stupid decisions. And let's largely ignore the flyover states…except for Nebraska. Come on, I can pick on one state.

As we begin, let's contemplate my Profound Thoughts as I began my three major trips.

No Cold Feet Allowed

I gave up my apartment and put my stuff in storage. Left my car at my parents' house. Stayed with my friend Kathy overnight. Had absolutely nowhere to sleep the next day except a college dorm in Pittsburgh. Let the multiple panics begin.

- Panic #1: As I mentioned, I was able to obtain a free Greyhound bus pass, but it was not in my possession. After several frantic phone calls with Rodney, the AT&T call center agent who took pity on me. I finally arranged a plan to pick it up.

- Panic #2: It is raining like crazy, but I had to pick up my bus pass without becoming a drowned rat. Kathy, help me! And she did.

- Panic #3: Coughing up a lung, and I'm supposed to start seeing our great nation in the morning. My son has insisted that "germs aren't real," but they sure felt real when I was sure I was dying and would end up at the emergency room rather than the airport.

- Panic #4: It seemed like a good idea at the time, but I have no idea why I had my wisdom teeth extracted before it was necessary. My twentysomething logic was that I would rather do it in my hometown rather than in a non-English-speaking nation. Unfortunately, I couldn't even yawn without my jaw hurting. On the other hand, yawning is optional and ibuprofen could be my friend.

London Calling

Wow, I need a passport. Am I officially a grownup? Or just a traveler wanting to visit a foreign country? Duh, the latter.

I figured it was easier to start my trip across the pond in a city that spoke English, albeit with a moderately amusing accent. After a brief respite in my hometown thanks to Kathy and her parents, here I go.

My backpack was even smaller than the one I used on my American travels. I didn't need no stinking sleeping bag, just a money belt for my passport and traveler's checks. No debit card or cell phone with appropriate SIM card. Bahaha!

Although I knew doing this trip was a big thing, there was no hesitation. I loved the parting words from a nice man I met at the Newark airport while awaiting my connection to London: "If you get into trouble, enjoy it." I loved the entire lyrics of Tom Petty's "American Girl" recorded in my journal, which reminded me that I was raised on promises. I loved my own mantra at this point: "I'll manage like I always do…somehow."

Don't Bring Me Down, Mom and Dad

I had returned to the left coast ready to change my life, become a famous writer, and generally implement the lofty goals I set for myself. However, I was relegated to pursuing my dubious goal of being a wage slave and enduring colleagues who privately laughed at me. At least I was making money and supporting myself. But I was bored.

My solution was to do it again, only better. Trains would be much more comfy than Greyhound buses. And now that I'd become experienced in locating cheap accommodations, I could sleep in actual beds more frequently. And this time, I would quit my job rather than taking a leave of absence. Colleagues, roll your eyes at how cute I was. A twentysomething who wanted to do stuff. Imagine that.

I put my stuff in storage again, and I'm still unclear why I bothered. It would have been cheaper to buy new stuff when I returned, rather than paying for garage sale crap to be stored in an overpriced facility. Couldn't bring it to my parents' house, though. I mean, I had my pride.

My parents were upset. Being a parent of three myself, I get it, but I did what I had to do. Dad dropped me off at my friend Dave's house and said, "I'm not gonna see you for three months and I don't want to hear it." Thanks for the encouragement.

As I grew up, Mom made it abundantly clear why my brother had more freedom than I did: "Because he's a boy." Thanks for the encouragement. Only boys can see the world; girls are destined to be barefoot, pregnant, and in the kitchen. Full disclosure: I have been all three of these at some point. But I was listening to Tom Petty and singing along throughout.

But here I go, even though I ended up in urgent care the next day. Oops, the wrong time to be barefoot. At least I wasn't pregnant and in the kitchen.

Yeah, This Is Better Than Working

You may notice that none of my adventures included national parks or tents. The simple explanation is that I had no car, no means to carry camping equipment, and no interest. I was content to patiently await my intermittent rooms with actual beds, reasonably clean bathrooms, and a door that usually locked.

Thanks to my husband, I have spent time in national parks and saw actual national wonders. However, my solo trips were not the time. And I was good with that.

I'm Not Dead, I'm in Pittsburgh

Here I am in Pittsburgh. I never dealt with people very well; getting the heck out of my hometown seemed very attractive.

Having overcome the drama, navel gazing, and intermittent panic before I started my adventure, it was an easy decision to choose my first destination. Two words: People Express. The bonus "attraction" was a Bad Boyfriend located within train distance. Cringing as I write this.

People Express was one of the first budget airlines. I mean, only $99 to fly coast to coast. They didn't even charge bag fees, and it was a nonstop flight. Are nonstop coast-to-coast flights even legal now?

In Pittsburgh, hooray! I'm really doing this! No matter that I'm still coughing up a lung and sneezing like crazy. Plus, my jaw hurts due to my too-soon wisdom teeth extraction and subsequent regret.

I stayed at the University of Pittsburgh dorm. I hope colleges still do this. Not fancy, but spacious and very pleasant.

Because I was a dumb and sheltered California girl, I wasn't sure about the city's air quality. I had heard the possibly apocryphal stories that the air was routinely so dark and smoky that streetlights automatically switched on in mid-afternoon. That the seriously polluted air ruined cars' paint jobs. Happily, even if those reports were correct, they were in the past. I could breathe with impunity.

And the city was intermittently gorgeous. In particular, my jaw dropped at the sight of the Three Rivers area—the confluence of, you guessed it, three rivers. In addition, the 1983 movie "Flashdance" prominently featured the Monongahela Incline Railway. Quick but scenic ride, with an observatory at the top. I loved channeling my inner Jennifer Beals as I began my ascent, even though I couldn't dance and wouldn't teasingly threaten to strip at the Pittsburgh nightclub at which her character performed. Like anybody would want to watch me do that.

Probably went to a museum or two. Stopped coughing and sneezing. Refrained from yawning.

As I walked around an apparently unsafe street before boarding my outbound bus, I wondered if the men thought I was a prostitute. In begrudging fairness to them, I was much closer to the city's iffy zone than I realized. And some of them perhaps wanted to think I was pathetic. Or desperate for cash.

Obviously, I didn't die. Good way to start a trip.

Lessons learned:

- Don't believe the disparaging media coverage about a city until I've seen it for myself.
- Determine a city's iffy zone and avoid it. Not hard.

Chattanooga Choo-Choo (ish)

I probably ended up in Chattanooga because of bus schedules that enabled me to sleep on an overnight run. As it turned out, I had an every-third-night room that may have astonishingly merited two stars. I also watched a great movie while in my jammies and experienced an unexpectedly fun outing.

Only God knows how I learned of the Lookout Mountain Incline Railway. I did not realize it at the time, but it has been in operation since 1895 and is one of the world's steepest passenger railways. Its summit elevation is nearly 2400 feet and as the name implies, the view at the top is priceless.

Instead of taking the easy way down, I decided it would be pleasant to walk back, just to say I did it. No, I didn't know the elevation, but you may have figured that out by now...the twentysomething lack-of-judgment thing.

More than halfway down, some motorist kindly offered to give me a ride and I accepted. Not smart, I know, but the walk was a lot longer than I expected. I obviously didn't die, and he didn't even hit on me. He was that day's Good Samaritan. Go him!

Settled into my room and ate a dinner that wasn't awful. Instead of overthinking it, I simply snuggled in my cozy bed and watched "Silkwood," a moving film starring Meryl Streep, while resting my sore legs. Yes, a Good Samaritan gave me a ride, but I still did the majority of the descent on foot.

Lesson (eventually) learned: Walking down from a summit always takes longer than it seems. I didn't completely learn that until after a 2009 hike in Yosemite National Park, throughout which I was convinced that I was destined to fall into the abyss and die a horribly gruesome death. Twentysomething Toni made reckless decisions, but 47-year-old Toni felt like an idiot. Will my kids ever forgive me for the ordeal? Fingers crossed.

This Bud's (Not) for Me

St. Louis wants to be a city, but doesn't know how. In spite of my sympathy, I enjoyed it in a pathetic frame of mind. I did see the Gateway Arch, which is awesome, although I will never understand why educated game show contestants have never heard of it. Not even Jeopardy contestants, who are generally much smarter than I.

Because some store clerks were rude, I decided to kill them with kindness. I would routinely say "Yes, sir" and "Yes, ma'am." But I'm a California girl; all we say is "Dude." I hope my unusually polite greetings resulted in a decent number of karma points.

I will never understand why I like brewery tours because I despise beer. Sorry, but it smells weird. The only explanation is that I enjoy seeing how things are made.

I've always been a sucker for tours, starting at a very young age. In second grade, the Kilpatrick's bakery field trip happened. OMG, the place smelled great, and everyone received a free pack of cinnamon rolls! My parents didn't even make me share them...or perhaps I devoured them immediately. It's been 52 years, for crissakes; I don't remember.

The Anheuser-Busch tour not only gave the group an inside look at the process, we also could see the ginormous Clydesdales up close and personal. Ginormous is probably an understatement. Plenty of my neighbors have horses, but the Clydesdales are unbelievable when greeting them face-to-face.

The tour was reasonably intriguing, but the hops room stunk to high heaven, and I was not the only one who felt that way. I cannot help but believe the tour guides were bemused by the tourists recoiling and literally holding their noses while in the room. Yes, it was that bad.

Lesson learned: I already knew I loved seeing how stuff is made, but I had to hold my nose at Anheuser-Busch. Ewww.

Next Time You See Memphis

I am a bad tourist when I visit Memphis. Despite two visits, I haven't still visited Graceland, and I assume Elvis Presley fans think that is a prosecutable offense, maybe even a felony. I ultimately did visit Sun Studios and the National Civil Rights Museum, but was relieved that neither was operating in 1985, so I was off the hook regarding skipping those back then. (For the sake of historical accuracy, Sun Studios began operations as the Memphis Recording Service in 1950, but did not become a tourist attraction until 1987.)

Because I didn't know what else to do, I decided to sign up for a low-wage gig at a random gospel music festival. Having enjoyed gospel choirs many times in New Orleans in previous years, I thought the festival would be a spiritual par-tay. I naively pictured my predominately Black brothers and sisters clapping their hands, dancing while singing, and making me excited to expand my spiritual horizons in a positively non-Catholic manner.

Bahaha.

Instead of clapping and singing along with an energized choir, I was reduced to selling carnations, feeling as if I were in a particularly somnolent Sunday service. At the very least, I was sure I wouldn't fall asleep because I was not allowed to sit down. I wondered why people couldn't splurge on a pleasant surprise for a spouse or friend. I wondered why I couldn't guilt people into buying my flowers by my sweaty and exhausted appearance.

That said, Memphis had a cheesy but ultimately super-cool attraction: Mud Island, which includes the Mississippi River Museum and the Mud Island River Park.

Cheesy aspect: Sorry Memphis, but the Mississippi River Museum is dumb. I'm not clear how many high school students seeking extra credit assembled the collection. Upside was that nobody goes there; I virtually had the place to myself.

Super-cool aspect: The Mud Island River Park, which is a walkable replica of the Mississippi River, complete with a scale-model river flow that incorporates actual water. I don't know who thought of it, but I enjoyed the paved walkway while absorbing too many fun facts about the history of the river. I could even wade in the shallow river if I chose to do so, but didn't want to get my shoes wet.

Apparently Mud Island isn't as popular as it used to be, and that makes me sad. There are several local musicians who perform there in the summer, and I hope some of the patrons walk the river replica while the opening act is doing their set.

History has always been my worst subject, but I learned so much about the Mighty Mississippi that I ultimately retained. Can't elementary schools schedule field trips to this place? They should, and teachers could even let the adventurous students get their shoes wet.

Lessons learned:

- Cities do gospel choirs differently. Unfortunately, Memphis didn't nail it.

- Need to seek out other river replicas. Is it possible the Memphis tourist commission is the only one who thought of this? If so, I am disappointed.

Do You Know What It Means to Miss New Orleans?

I first went to New Orleans in 1984 for the World's Fair. I will never understand why I still love a city in which many unfortunate things happened to me. No details needed, but I survived and ultimately learned my lessons, albeit the hard way. Lived there for almost two years.

Yes, I know that in the minds of many, the city is synonymous with Mardi Gras. However, it has so many artsy and magical aspects. And the food. OMG, the food.

While enjoying the ride on the historic St. Charles streetcar, I noticed some, um, unusual street names in succession: Polymnia,

Melpomene, Calliope, Clio, Euterpe, Terpsichore, Thalia, Urania, Erato. Whatever.

However, I subsequently found out these nine streets are known as the "Muses Streets." Wait, what? Was it too hard to name the streets after American presidents or to simply name them in numerical sequence? Apparently it was indeed too hard for Barthelomy Lafon; he had to go the esoteric route.

A resident of France, Monsieur Lafon arrived in the city after a 1788 fire nearly devastated the city. A respected architect, he played an instrumental role in the city's rebuild and apparently thought it would be artsy and amusing to name nine streets after the Greek muses, who were believed to provide ongoing inspiration to artists of various persuasions. I can picture him saying, "Bahaha, I can't wait to see how the city's residents mangle the pronunciations." Yep, many do. To this day, I'm unclear about the correct pronunciation of Melpomene. Which syllable receives the emphasis?

I imagine he had much more fun implementing these street names than taking the lazy route of Jackson St., Washington St., and Louisiana Ave. Unfortunately, those are actually streets in the same neighborhood. Other architects surely gossiped among themselves in subsequent years. "Bahaha, we sure showed Lafon."

The city's official motto is *"laissez les bon temps rouler"* ("let the good times roll"). Reason for a parade? Any day that ends in y. Reason for a festival? Food. Reason for a job? Income, but punctuality is optional.

New Orleans has been characterized as the "most European city in America," and I cannot argue. Go to a tiny grocery store and engage in a debate about the best gosh-darn andouille sausage in town. Go to any self-respecting restaurant on Monday for red beans and rice. And OMG, muffulettas. Two words: Central Grocery. Decatur St. In the French Quarter. Best sandwich on the planet. No, they are not paying me to say this.

Newbie residents of the Quarter are somewhat "fondly" referred to as Quarter Rats (there is now a band of that name…who knew?). I am unclear how this term originated, but I wasn't one while I lived there. Or maybe I was. I was so young.

I have the dubious honor of meeting not one, but two Bad Boyfriends there. I also have the actual honor of seeing Dr. John (ask your elders) at a free concert, as well as witnessing Mardi Gras in a family-friendly setting on St. Charles Avenue, one of the major parade routes. Because I lived a block off St. Charles for a while, I could watch from my apartment or simply walk for two minutes. And not have to find a parking space!

Lessons learned:

- New Orleans is a wonderful place, in spite of Bad Boyfirends who are waaay too easy to meet.
- Never nap in public, no matter how tired I was. Again, my kids may be reading, so I won't repeat the details. But it wasn't my fault.
- Indeed, hell hath no fury like a woman scorned. I will take the story of how I learned this lesson to my grave.
- Eat muffulettas as often as possible. My family returned to the city in 2014, and we left our Central Grocery in the fridge when we left for the airport. I have never figured out what was wrong with us.

Margaritaville

Am I allowed to go to Key West even if I'm not a Jimmy Buffett fan? Trust me, this is a funny joke. Even if you're not cracking up, I am.

It is the southernmost point of the United States, and a large statue confirms the exact location of said point. But they aren't exaggerating about how far south it is; it was probably a six-hour bus ride from Miami. Very scenic ride, but very long. And very worth it.

When I arrived, I found a suitable zero-star room and set off to explore. Although it is not a small town, the area of interest to tourists is very walkable. It immediately reminded me of New Orleans' French Quarter, only with roaming cute lizards rather than menacing palmetto bugs. Trust me, palmetto bugs are large and disgusting. If you haven't seen one with your own eyes, lucky you.

The main drag is Duval Street, which was a slightly more benign rendition of New Orleans' Bourbon Street. The big hook for tourists was that Ernest Hemingway drank here. The town tries to playfully promote this narrative via Sloppy Joe's bar, the logo of which includes his face. At least they also have an annual Hemingway lookalike contest, during which I assume alcohol consumption is optional.

As I have learned, Hemingway had two Key West endeavors aside from drinking and writing:

- Big-game fishing. After buying his own boat, he pioneered new techniques to quickly catch and reel in super-big fish before the circling shark(s) caught wind of his plans. He subsequently became a vice president of the International

Game Fish Association. No, I hadn't heard of it either, but it is indeed a thing.

- Criticizing the local government after the federal government's inadequate response to a 1935 hurricane, which killed 423 residents depending on the source. After the hurricane, he used his own boat to pull bodies out of the ocean.

A lesser hook was that President #33 Harry Truman's Little White House, his summer respite, was here. It greatly increased my respect for both of them. Is there a more beautiful place to drink or summer?

I mostly chilled all day because summer in the Keys is very hot. I snuck into a fancy hotel, then sat, reclined, and napped in their pool. (Trust me, you can nap in a pool, but you had to be there.) The pool water was actually more comfortable than the Gulf of Mexico, the water of which felt like a bathtub. No joke.

I decided to do a snorkeling tour, which was a new experience. I was pleased that the tour operators distributed flotation devices to ensure the participants would not die an unceremonious death for which they would be held liable.

The tropical fish were adorable. They were oblivious to the giant creature swimming with them (that would be me), quickly figured out I was not their enemy, and resumed their lives. It was as if they knew the Key West vibe and acted accordingly.

Mallory Pier is the location of a unique gathering enjoyed by locals and tourists alike: observing nightly sunset. Some locals would attempt to monetize the gathering by selling cookies and/or panhandling, but of course somebody always wants to monetize locations at which gullible tourists congregate. In spite of my cynical nature, I loved witnessing how a simple sunset could be so celebrated. Among the locals, there was even regular agreement to "meet me at sunset."

It rains in Key West. Duh. However, only wimps use umbrellas. If I used one, I might as well have carried a sign: "Look, I'm a tourist pretending to belong here, but I don't want to get wet." However, with the heat and humidity of summer, the rain proved to be an opportunity to hose off and refresh without having to actually take my clothes off and get in the shower.

How the heck did I end up walking in a cemetery at midnight during a violent rainstorm? No TV, insomnia, boredom, all of the above? On the basis of a decision that seemed better suited for a horror movie plot, there I was. It was surreal. No ghosts. No psycho chasing me with a chainsaw. But I never did it again. Anywhere.

Lessons learned:

- Although I loved walking through a cemetery at midnight in the pouring rain, there was no reason to repeat that experience. I mean, the psycho-chasing-me-with-a-chainsaw thing.

- Even if I declined to use an umbrella in Key West, I used them elsewhere. I don't like to get wet.

More Than a Feeling

I accidentally arrived in Boston during a huge celebration for the Celtics' 16th basketball championship. I had just exited the bus station, bleary-eyed, simply expecting to prepare for the night's Red Sox game, but wow and hooray. Such a happy surprise.

Heck, I'm not even a basketball fan, but imagine a million people in downtown. Imagine a fist-pumping Bill Walton on a parade float sporting a Grateful Dead T-shirt. A more subdued but clearly thrilled Larry Bird. Other players I didn't know, but they were certainly ecstatic, as were the parade attendees. My favorite sign: "NBA championships are like women…the 16th is as good as the first."

As a brief digression, it was fascinating read Walton's obituary. After he passed away fairly recently, I learned that he might have been the greatest player in college basketball history and was on two NBA championship teams. After retiring, he became an Emmy-winning broadcaster in spite of his pronounced stutter. His famous quote: "Playing basketball with Larry Bird is like singing with Jerry Garcia," referencing the co-founder of the Grateful Dead.

But back to Boston.

As is the case for most people, I needed to eat. I randomly encountered Flash's, the greasiest of greasy spoons. Because I stayed in an iffy part of town as I usually did, there were no chain restaurants. I crossed my fingers and entered.

The staff were brothers. As brothers can be sometimes, they were alternatively sweet and gruff to one another. And gosh, their food! I don't know if they are still open, but I doubt they are/were the type of operation to create a website even if they are still in business.

Lessons learned:

- Stumbling into a ginormous parade is exciting.

- I don't need no stinking McDonald's as long as establishments such as Flash's are an option. Overhearing the fraternal squabbling was a strangely poignant bonus.

Gator on the Lawn

Of course, I couldn't claim to be Tom Petty's Number One Fan if I didn't go to Gainesville.

Elvis Presley fans go to Graceland. Beatles fans go to Liverpool. Prince fans go to Minneapolis. No idea where Taylor Swift fans go.

Tom Petty fans go to Gainesville, Florida. Regrettably, I met a Gainesville resident in recent years who gives fans a thorough tour of Tom's world, but I didn't know him back then. I was on my own.

Shockingly, I didn't run into Tom having breakfast at the local greasy spoon (of course not; he was rich and famous…and on tour.) I didn't know to seek out Dub's Bar or Mudcrutch Farm, some early venues for his band, the Heartbreakers. But hey, I can find something. Somewhere.

I decided to look up Tom's dad in the telephone book chained to the interior of a phone booth. I know, I know…what's a telephone book and what's a phone booth?

Once upon a time, there were no smartphones. To contact someone while out and about, you had to find a phone booth (which was not hard), close the door in the hopes that claustrophobia didn't set in (they were small), put actual coins in the phone's slot, and have an actual spoken conversation. (Texting? Bahaha.) You also had to know the phone number of the person you were calling rather than accessing your contact list. After that, you needed to walk home barefoot in the snow. Okay, I'm getting carried away.

However, the chained telephone book provided a resource to locate someone's phone number if necessary. Although there was an option to have an unlisted number, most people were okay with being listed.

Having not done my research about notable Heartbreakers' notable Gainesville locales in the early days, I was reduced to looking up Tom's dad, Earl, in the telephone book. And whaddaya know, he was listed. The father of a famous rock star and I could just call him and say, "Hello Earl, this is Toni. May I please speak to Tom?"

No, I didn't, but being the dorky fan that I was, and am, I got a huge kick out of seeing Earl's entry. I contemplated ripping the page out of the book as a souvenir, but didn't do that either. My reasoning at the time, I suppose, was that ripping out a page was a prosecutable offense, comparable to removing the "Do Not Remove Under Penalty of Law" tag from a mattress.

As I wandered around Gainesville after my phone booth encounter, I noticed that every other business appeared to have "Gator" in the name, and I quickly figured out that it was an homage to the University of Florida Gators. Remarkably, even the renowned sports beverage — yes, Gatorade — was created in Gainesville at the university. They sure love their Gator references in those parts. Tom's music publishing company was even titled "Gone Gator Music."

Of course, I had to buy a T-shirt that ostensibly promoted the city's Gator Surf Shop, even though there was no business with that actual name. And I don't think there was surfing in Gainesville, but I could be wrong.

I do know that I loved pretending I was walking down a street Tom may also have walked on. And I loved pretending that maybe Tom happened to be in town that day. Maybe we would run into one another, enjoy a leisurely lunch, and discuss his next album.

Lesson learned: Nothing wrong with being a fangirl occasionally. It had happened in previous years and would happen again in subsequent years. Tom's dad lived at 1715 Northeast 6th Terrace. I didn't even have to consult my journal to remember that.

Somewhere Under Heaven

Have to start with a prequel.

My family's annual vacation was to Lake Tahoe, Nevada. At the time, Nevada was the only state with legalized gambling. Dad would gamble, Mom would pretend to gamble but instead pocket the ostensible gambling money, and we kids would hang out at the beach and eat the fast food we were allowed one week each year. We also attended a dinner show at a casino, which usually featured a reasonably famous singer or comedian.

The casino wasn't kidding when they emphasized the "dinner" aspect of the dinner show. Even though I was only a tween…OMG, the abalone. Absolutely nobody can prepare abalone without overcooking it. I hope the Harrah's Casino chef ultimately got a cooking show on the Food Network, Netflix, or some other foodie showcase.

The next day, three of the four kids were enjoying King's Beach while Mom and my sister went for a stroll. They ran into TONY EFFING BENNETT! The guy we were seeing later that night! Just walking on the beach like a mere mortal!

As my sister tells it, Mom's head exploded, just as I would if I encountered Tom Petty on a random beach before a show. In astonishment, she simply shouted, "TONY!" And he very kindly responded, "How are you today?"

I wish I had encountered a random celebrity on a beach at some point, even if it wasn't Tom Petty. So happy Mom had that experience.

Moving on, let's have fun at the awesome places before I rant about the awful ones in the next chapter.

My Old Kentucky Home (For a Day or So)

Somehow I made it to the Kentucky Derby in Louisville. It is always held on the first Saturday in May; the weather was quite pleasant although May is usually the state's rainiest month. Go Louisville!

The day before the race, I was able to wander around Churchill Downs, site of the Derby, on my own. It's just a big horse racing venue, but it was such a kick to have it virtually to myself.

I was able to wander into the betting booth and pretend I was one of the staff who processed bets on the races. Nobody locked these places up? On the other hand, how many twentysomething women want to pretend they work for a racetrack? Perhaps securing it was more trouble than it was worth…nothing to steal. But someone randomly surfaced who snapped a photo of me at the ticket booth (no selfie sticks back then). Thanks, random stranger.

Derby Day was quite the spectacle, with many women wearing fancy, over-the-top hats, a tradition that dates back to the 19th century. And apparently it is a requirement that all entrants indulge in a mint julep in a commemorative glass. Okay, if I must. Unfortunately, my glass broke during my subsequent travels. It was so cute and commemorative. Sigh.

Of course, I had to buy a cheap ticket, which enabled me to stand in the infield with a bunch of other financially challenged fans rather than to sit in an actual seat.

As the day began, an apparently local band performed "My Old Kentucky Home" for the crowd, and many people sang along. Because Tom Petty never covered it, I was not able to sing along, but it was very poignant in a sporting-event way. I had no idea about the traditions associated with a simple horse race, but enjoyed experiencing them.

Time to moderately focus on the races. I bet a big $2 on Spend a Buck just because I liked his name. I then made my way to the infield where some fans were wearing beer can boxes as hats. In spite of the curious and amusing headgear, people were just having a good time with no inappropriate conduct or public drunkenness. I made a couple of fast friends, but declined to wear a beer can box. I mean, I had my dignity.

It was finally time for the Big Event after the completion of the opening races. Somehow I was able to watch after climbing up to the top of a porta-potty. One guy provided comic relief with his comment that "if these collapse, we're gonna be in deep sh*t." Another guy asked me to marry him, bahaha.

From my perch, I got a perfect view of Spend a Buck as he sped by. Of course it happened quickly, but Derby Day was all about the party. And Spend a Buck won, woohoo! I could finally afford that breakfast I was saving up for.

At the end of the day, I joined many other financially challenged attendees on a bus back to downtown Louisville. It was a fairly long ride and we were crammed together. We passed the time by making Peoria jokes.

For the uninitiated, Peoria, Illinois, was long considered to be the quintessential town whose population was considered to be representative of our nation. If someone had a new product, the dilemma was "Will it sell in Peoria?" If someone had a political concept, the dilemma was "Will it play in Peoria?"

As we approached our destination, it was unclear why were we laughing like crazy at Peoria jokes. But we laughed like crazy, which was the point.

I don't think anyone from Peoria was on the bus. We weren't making fun of them, just the concept of them and their dubious significance to the overall American state of mind.

Lessons learned:

- Witnessing traditions was great, even without knowing their origins.
- Cheap tickets are great, especially because I didn't have to spend money for an ostentatious hat.
- Never miss an opportunity to laugh like crazy, even if the jokes are bad.

Learning to Fry

Who knew Louisville would be worthy of two—count 'em, two—vignettes? But a museum dedicated to a fast-food joint seemed cheesy enough to work.

The Kentucky Fried Chicken Museum no longer exists, apparently replaced by the Harland Sanders Cafe. But Colonel Harland Sanders was a chicken pioneer who combined the legendary eleven herbs and spices to make some seriously great chicken...years ago. I wonder who lost the recipe to the seriously great chicken. These days, ewww. We desperately ate at KFC in 2021 after an extremely long day, and it was awful. Take that, YUM Brands! The real Colonel Sanders must be rolling over in his grave.

I had some time on my hands and decided to venture out to the museum. What a fun place! I was simultaneously amused and appalled by the TV ads intended for Asian countries that portrayed Colonel Sanders with slanted eyes. Racist much? These ads have vanished somewhere in the memory hole, which is probably a good thing.

Thankfully, the film loop of other old commercials was inoffensive. One showed Paul Revere shouting, "The chicken is coming!" The tagline was "Why should you be making dinner when you could be making history?" Someone deserved a raise for that one.

It was so entertaining to learn the history of a quasi-colonel. The only disappointment was that there were no free samples. Remember, KFC tasted good back then.

Lesson learned: Cheesy museums can be a blast. I never knew when something would unexpectedly crack me up.

Lesson not learned by YUM Brands: For shame. Even the formerly great biscuits are awful these days.

Never Mind the Bollocks

As you will see in the next chapter, I thought "Cats" was dumb. However, I'd somehow found out that Chicago's Steppenwolf Theater was a destination. Very artsy, but not to the extent of being intimidating for a decidedly uncool person. That would be me.

Their production was titled "Vicious;" it was the semi-true chronicle of the last days of the life of Sid Vicious of the Sex Pistols. (Ask your elders, especially about the title of this vignette.)

I dressed as if I were going on a hike, but nobody really seemed to care. That said, I wished I looked as stylish and artsy as some of the attendees there. Truth be told, though, I never look stylish and artsy. Even now, when I have money. I have officially become Steve Jobs (black shirt and jeans). I wish I were kidding. But back to the Steppenwolf.

Tiny, tiny venue. It was certainly bigger than my living room, but not by much.

George Clooney portrayed Sid's drug dealer. Even though he was a working actor at the time, he was not at the time as famous as he has become. Such a commanding stage presence, but I didn't even know who he was. (I didn't watch "The Facts of Life"...okay, maybe a couple of times.) I am not surprised that he became as successful as he has. Other Steppenwolf alumni are John Malkovich, Laurie Metcalf, and Gary Sinise; you've probably heard of at least one of them.

Great and moving show. Much better than "Cats."

My kids are still reasonably impressed by my "Vicious" program that lists Clooney in the cast. Furthermore, all three of them were theater kids, which added more to my bragging rights. It's great when I can impress the moderately jaded, especially when they are my own kids.

Lesson learned: I never knew when I might see someone perform before they became somebody.

The New Colossus and a Par-Tay

Although I was too bored in history class to absorb it, the Statue of Liberty was gifted to our nation from France in 1885. I did retain that it was restored in 1984, so go me! The big par-tay to celebrate the restoration happened in July 1986.

I don't remember the majestic sailing boats. I don't remember the music concert or fireworks. Because I was always on a serious budget, staying in New York City was not an option. Instead, I wandered the streets in broad daylight and had a blast. Because the streets were devoid of cars and taxicabs, pedestrians could walk anywhere they wanted. We didn't need no stinking sidewalks.

I bought a commemorative T-shirt from one of the random vendors. Because it was horribly hot that day, wearing it was just too much. It was a cheap and thin; I have no idea why I thought taking it off would make me feel more comfortable and less sweaty. But I did.

A group of New Yorkers (I assume) were walking behind me. Their loud response: "Whoa, you're gonna make us hurt ourselves!" I had to laugh; I was just hot, not staging a daytime strip show. And definitely not topless.

I continued walking along the car-free streets and it was weird in a fun way....or fun in a weird way. I paid someone to take a photo of me as a pretend Statue of Liberty, then got the heck out of town in search of accommodations I could afford.

Lesson learned: Celebrations can play out in a manner I'd never expected. I wish I'd saved that cheap T-shirt, but it probably disintegrated within a week.

Hooray, Something Rotten

London was a great place to begin my time across the pond. Upon my groggy arrival after my delightfully cheap red-eye flight, I needed to find a room. Remember, this was the dark ages of no internet, plus long-distance calls that cost a king's ransom.

Thankfully, it didn't take too long to find a place. I was sure I only had hours before serious jet lag kicked in. After a few tries, I found a room that was roughly the size of a large closet, with no private bathroom. As usual, it was not the greatest neighborhood, but was conveniently located near Victoria Station and was cozy enough. Not at all frightening, and I could go to sleep as early as I wanted. And I was in effing London; I didn't care if my room would never be pictured in a high-end travel publication.

After a serious night's sleep, I did the obligatory Round London bus tour. Good overview of the city, and I could postpone navigating the subway system. I just had to park myself on a double-decker bus and seem interested.

When I braved the subway the next day, officially named the London Underground but unofficially and amusingly nicknamed the "Tube," I was amused by its recurring announcement: "Mind the gap!" Its intent was to remind passengers that some stations had gaps between the boarding platforms and the Tube trains. I didn't see how the proverbial gap could kill anyone, but I suppose it may have been a problem for women wearing stiletto heels.

Tourist attractions, okay. More accurately, blah blah blah.

However, I was determined to not do the tourist thing. Yes, I am a temporary Londoner! I thankfully met a local musician and he suggested a visit to the King's Head, a seriously headbanging club at which his band was performing.

The music was good enough, but I was baffled by how many patrons knew I was an American. Sure, I have an American accent, but how would they know that if I'm not talking? My sunny-ish attitude? My unfortunate wardrobe choice while in a world-class city? My good teeth and gums?

I had to make sure I filled up on the (fortunately) over-the-top breakfasts. In a pinch, I could suck it up and tolerate steak and kidney pie, but gosh. I couldn't help but wonder if the American Revolution started because the Founding Fathers simply got tired of eating crappy food. I hope and assume the food is better now, but not back then.

The best thing about London was that live theater was actually affordable. I could purchase a ticket to William Shakespeare's "Hamlet" without skipping meals the next day.

Of course we all know that the Bard wrote like a pompous ass just because he could. Nooo! I had read "Hamlet" in college, but the live rendition was truly funny, at least when unfortunate deaths weren't occurring. Hamlet's dad haunting him from beyond the grave was especially hilarious. Shakespeare was ultimately a lowbrow in spite of his sometimes intimidating language, which was probably his running joke in an attempt to convince his future readers to think he was actually a snob.

Repertory theatre was even better. I was entertained and educated while watching "Rat in the Skull," a performance about the Irish Nationalist criminals incarcerated during The Troubles in Northern Ireland. Please refer to "No Jokes Allowed" for the unfortunate and sad details.

Fast forward to 2013. Recovering from jet lag was much easier when I was younger. After arriving in London as a twentysomething, I simply went to sleep, exhausted, at 6 PM, and was ready to roll the next day. When I and my family went to Italy 28 years later, it took me a gosh-darn week to get a good night's sleep. This was after I assured the family we would be fine the next day. Exactly what did I know? Actually, nothing. I thought I would adapt to jet lag as I did in Back in the Day. Bahaha! My husband and kids listened to me in disbelief. Then slept.

Lessons learned:

- London is fun, even if it's not sunny California and even if everything shuts down at 11:00 PM.
- Affordable theatre, OMG!
- Mind the gap. Just in case.

All Shakespeare, All the Time

It was a bigger pain getting to Stratford-Upon-Avon, Shakespeare's hometown, than I expected, but I survived.

After studying his works in college, I expected the Bard's hometown to be a quiet and bucolic place populated by tourists--

most likely English or literature majors--quietly walking the streets while silently reciting his greatest sonnets.

Bahaha! It was a circus.

It was so big and so overrun by tourists, including quite a few punk rocker types who had hair I am afraid to try sporting. I clung to the hope that after the day trippers left, I could explore the city in peace.

Just as Liverpool is about the Beatles, Stratford is about Will. I got a huge dose of Bardmania, but his grave was especially intriguing because of the epitaph he wrote for himself. I have written my own, but you know it's not nearly as good. I didn't come up with it myself; it consists of a Tom Petty lyric. Gone Gator Music, sue me when I'm dead.

Of course, the city staged his plays. Because it is my shortcoming that I must read his plays before I can appreciate a live performance, I thought "The Merry Wives of Windsor" was forgettable. On the other hand, I was convinced they watered it down for the tourists. Did I say there were a lot of tourists?

That said, it was great to walk the streets he did. Sigh.

Lesson learned: Robert Graves, a British novelist and poet, nailed it when he famously said that "A remarkable thing about Shakespeare is that he is really very good, in spite of all the people who say he is very good."

All Beatles, Nearly All the Time

Of course, a visit to Liverpool is a pilgrimage for Beatles fans. I am somewhat of a Beatles fan (my favorite was George), but as you already know, Tom Petty is my guy. Tom and George became best friends and bandmates in the Traveling Wilburys, but I'm sure Tom wouldn't fear I shifted my loyalty. Especially because the Wilburys didn't exist at the time.

It's not unreasonable to assume Liverpool tourism would be based on "BEATLES! BEATLES! BEATLES! They played here! John slept here! Paul had lunch here! George wrote songs here! Ringo did, um, something here." But I was surprised at how well the city presented their legacy without making it look cheesy and pandering. And Ringo is great; I really don't mean to join the pundits who were so condescending. But I guess I just did. Sorry, Ringo.

Bus tour. The Cavern Club, where they first played. The Jacaranda, another club they played. The record store that inspired Dire Straits' song "Money for Nothing." (Mark Knopler actually heard the quote "the little [you-know-what] with the earring and the makeup" at that store. At least, that's what the tour guide told us.)

After the bus tour, I was off to Beatle City (which has apparently been renamed or reimagined). An actual historian must have curated the exhibit because it really gave me insight into their roots. But wait, there's more.

I had a not-too-awful room--maybe one-star--and there was a musical based on the career of Elvis Presley right down the street: "Are You Lonesome Tonight?" Once again, I didn't have to mortgage my house (had I owned one) to enjoy live entertainment. Go Britain!

The show's premise was that old, overweight Elvis was watching movies of young, svelte Elvis, while wondering what the heck happened. I was ultimately surprised it didn't achieve more success, especially due to his untimely death and the sheer number of Elvis impersonators that experienced careers with varying success.

It was very poignant. Perhaps as the theatrical Elvis watched his younger self, he was struck by his coulda-woulda-shoulda regrets. And so was I. I teared up.

Lesson learned: Liverpool did it right. Although the Powers That Be were undoubtedly aware of the reason most tourists visit, no cynical pandering to fans was allowed.

Take Me to the River

Off to Mainz, West Germany, located a manageable distance from Frankfurt. I only went there because one of my Bad Boyfriends suggested it.

After I arrived, I surmised why he liked it. Porn magazines sold on the street, as well as red-light districts signaling houses of prostitution in abundance. I was surprised and appalled by how the sex trade was openly practiced throughout West German cities at the time (hopefully it has changed). In our nation at the time, people would at least have to venture into a marginal and possibly dangerous neighborhood for porn or prostitutes. Of course, that was pre-internet.

I stayed in a way-too-fancy hotel because I was due for a break from zero-star hovels. Wow, American hotel brands are waaay overpriced in other nations. Regardless, after sleeping in a seriously comfy bed, I was off to a cruise on the Rhine River.

Cruising the Rhine is one of my fondest memories. Ancient castles on the shore, affordable refreshments, beautiful day, the best

Gewurztraminer I've ever had for a very reasonable price. Because Rick Steves had not blessed Mainz as an Official Tourist Destination, I didn't have to talk to anybody, eavesdrop on Americans discussing the stock market, or listen to irritating loudspeaker commentary telling me why the stuff I was witnessing was So Important and Historical. Instead, the vibe was hi-relax-enjoy-the-scenery. And I did.

Aside from the gorgeous, gorgeous Rhine River, West Germany and I didn't get along. Why? Because everyone spoke English and there was no challenging language barrier to overcome? Because there were so few entitled men on whom to unleash my aggressions? Because I was tired of feeling sanctimonious about the pervasiveness of porn and red-light districts?

At any rate, the Rhine. All is forgiven. And I could rest assured that plenty of entitled men awaited during my remaining time in West Germany. Still shaking my head at the memory of Wolfgang, the train passenger on a weekend pass from prison. The one who thought I was gullible enough to sponsor him for American citizenship

Lessons learned:

- Didn't love West Germany overall, but OMG the Rhine.
- Bad Boyfriends are occasionally good for something.

Into the Arena

Freddie Mercury of Queen sang an opera song titled "Barcelona" with Montserrat Caballe, an opera singer with a serious set of pipes. "Bohemian Rhapsody" was just a warmup. Even if opera does not interest you, Freddie's attire is so distinguished as the duo captivates the audience. Broadening musical horizons is good, and nobody has a monopoly on talent.

Bullfighting has been banned in the province of Catalonia, the region in which Barcelona is located...something about the inherent unkindness of entertainment that involves animal cruelty. I honestly respect the bull advocates for their efforts, but witnessing an actual event was far different than I expected.

Before attending the Barcelona *corrida* (bullfight) at the Plaza del Toros, I simply pictured a bunch of spectators shouting *"Toro! Toro! Toro!"* (not to be confused with the 1970 movie "Tora! Tora! Tora!," which dramatized the 1941 Pearl Harbor attack). It was anything but.

To start things off, the event featured the *picadors* (bullfighters on horseback), the appearance of whom is analogous to the pregame show of any sporting event. Their job was to chase and taunt the bull, presumably until he got tired. I guess?

The *picadors* were ultimately entertainers, exciting the spectators while not putting themselves in significant danger. On the other hand, being in a ring with a huge animal that could randomly kill one of them at any moment sounds like significant danger to me.

As the *picadors* were fulfilling their pregame show roles, the spectators were gorging on junk food, shouting *"Ole, ole, ole!"* (the *"Toro"* chant was apparently my dumb American assumption) and optimistically assuming the *picador* would probably not die.

Souvenirs were cute. The *banderillas* (decorated wooden sticks with spiked ends) were reminiscent of the weapon used to kill the bull. As you read on, I have attended many baseball games, but none of the merch included theoretically lethal weapons. But let's continue.

After the bull was sufficiently winded, in came the *matador*—the guy whose job was to kill him. I expected to see the equivalent of a linebacker-type macho man who was there to finish the job the wimpy *picadors* could not. But no.

The *matador* was revered, almost a sex symbol. He entered the ring and enticingly brandished his cape, as much at the bull as at the spectators. Maybe every girl didn't go nuts, but I sure did. This, I was certain, was what macho looked like. "See how brave I am! No stinking bull will vanquish me!" He obviously meant and believed that.

Not-so-fun fact: In the past 300 years, over 500 *matadors* were killed during their efforts. I am very thankful I did not have to witness such a horrible event, but it does remind me that the *matadors* were not engaging in child's play.

Fast forward to 2013. In Arles, France, there was no bullfighting, just "bull games." The French bull games were referred to as the *Camargue*, with hopefully no carnage involved, just the goal to pluck a ribbon from between the bull's horns. In my mind, it was still dangerous; we are talking about bull vs. man. And the bull is bigger.

Unlike the Barcelona *corridas*, the French bull games publicize the name of the bull rather than that of the *raseteur* (somewhat comparable to a *matador*). The bull was the star...really? And if the bull kills the *raseteur*, he can never compete again! Completely different vibe.

Don't hate me, but it was more exciting when the bull actually died. The French *raseteur* wasn't nearly as alluring. His job was just as risky, but it looked a bit pathetic compared to Barcelona's *matadors*. I assume he had a boss to answer to. And he had to acknowledge that time marches on. Regardless of historical precedent, our world had evolved beyond watching animals killed for entertainment value. I accept that.

But gosh, it was so benign. Whenever the bull taunted the pregame show guys (what are they called in French?), they would jump up on the barrier to escape. They didn't need no stinking macho. It was much more exciting to watch the Barcelona *matador* taunt the bull to bring it on already, play to the crowd with his enticing cape, then move in for the kill. PETA, I appreciate your efforts, but the actual *corrida* was so much better. I think many football games exhibit more bloodthirsty emotions.

Lesson learned: I admit I am a horrible person, but it was quite exciting to see the *matador* emerge with the bulls' ears when his mission was accomplished. And he certainly worked it. Bullfighting has been banned in much of our world, but the real thing was exciting. Okay, I will duck now.

Where Are the Two Gentlemen?

I wanted to continue my jaded cynicism when I arrived in Verona, Italy. As you probably know, it was the fictional setting of Shakespeare's "Romeo and Juliet" (come on, you've heard of this play) and "The Two Gentlemen of Verona." When I arrived, I quickly became enchanted.

The Giardino Giusti consists of some ancient ruins that were converted to a public garden (albeit with an admission charge...not exactly "public"). After I climbed a tower's spiral staircase, I enjoyed hearing church bells in the distance. Priests and nuns strolling everywhere. I simply had to exclaim, "Romeo, Romeo, wherefore art thou Romeo?"

I appreciated that Verona didn't attempt to overhype the Shakespeare aspect; they just let the town speak for itself. And it did. I supplied the color commentary in my mind.

Lesson learned: I never knew when some towns are going to be absolutely gorgeous, tourist angle be damned. I wanna go back to Verona.

"My Own Sun" Sounds Prettier in Italian

Naples. Sigh. Long pause.

"O Sole Mio" ("My Own Sun") is a classic Neopolitan song that was performed by famous deceased Italian singers such as Enrico Caruso and Luciano Pavarotti. I had vaguely heard of the song because Mom was a Caruso fan, but was otherwise clueless. That said, I came to understand why Naples deserved its own national-ish anthem.

Of course, the traditional Italy trajectory consists of Rome, Florence, and Venice. But Naples. My guess was that because I am full-blooded Sicilian, I could better relate to Italian culture the further south I traveled.

Yep.

Naples is glorious chaos. Because I didn't die attempting to cross the street (which I almost did, but I could save my life by hiding behind the locals crossing at the same time), I simply basked in the ambience after eating amazing food. No such thing as bad food in Italy, not even the cheapie stuff at the train station.

Museums, okay. Unbelievably, the National Archeological Museum has a porn room (officially known as the *Gabinetto Secretto*—the Secret Cabinet). It displays the sexually themed objects recovered from Pompeii and Herculaneum, two nearby sites buried under volcanic ash in AD 79. I didn't blush, but it sure was weird.

Museums aside, navigating the city was an, um, adventure. After taking a bus, I could appreciate how a sardine feels.

That said, *Spaccanapoli* (the main street of Naples' historic center) was an incredible zoo of a neighborhood. Prayed that the guy driving his Vespa on the sidewalk didn't run me over. Made friends with an Italian family whose street market sold eggs. If there was any doubt regarding the eggs' lineage, I could meet, greet, and pet the chickens who laid them.

If I was in a bad mood, I just needed to watch the Italian men for a while. They were silly in a sweet way with their pot bellies, bald heads, open flies, ill-fitting and unmatched clothes. *La dolce vita* for sure…they didn't need no stinking diets or stylish clothes. Because Naples has the best food on the planet, it was more practical for them to wear their ill-fitting pants and indulge in the *frittatina di pasta, cassatine siciliane, cannoli* shells filled to order, and pizza pizza pizza! When is the last time you ate an entire pizza without feeling like a hopeless glutton? In Naples, it was sharing a pizza that was odd.

Aside from the visuals, I loved the random acts of kindness. Heck, I was only in town for three days, but the espresso bar guys remembered that I didn't like sugar in my coffee. And the espresso bar's mascot—an adorable puppy—kept me company while he devoured the crumbs and leftovers on the sidewalk. It was strangely and poignantly comforting.

And then there was Cammiso Pasquale, the man in charge of the street market that sold the extremely fresh eggs. I took a photo of him and his chickens. Because he wanted a copy of it, I mailed it to him when I returned to the US and developed my film. Yes, that is really how you had to share photos in 1985.

And then there was the nameless man who helped me out in a moment of souvenir panic. I had finally found some Genuine Italian Bedsheets and tried to mail them to my sister. Of course, the postal worker laughed in disbelief at the stupid American and told me there was no way she could ship them without the proper packaging. Although I had resigned myself to schlepping them home in my too-small backpack, the nameless man escorted me to a some-kind-of-business that could package and ship them. He didn't even hit on me; he was just doing his good deed for the day

And then there were the streets. What a joy it was to walk the streets and see them teeming with people laughing, gabbing, playing cards, doing anything that didn't involve watching bad TV and wondering why they were lonely. Here I am in a dive of a city, a mostly poor city, and I saw joy. And we Americans think we have it all figured out.

Time to call Mom and Dad. In Naples' pre-internet dark ages, I had to go to a "telephone office" to make an international call and wait three hours—I wish I were exaggerating—until the call finally connected. At the very least, the office attendant didn't offer me a lame and false reason for the delay; he simply shrugged to convey that "only God knows why this is taking so long." While I (im)patiently waited, some random guy invited me to fly to Tunisia with him. Really.

Fast forward to 2013. I returned to Naples, this time with my family, and was absolutely astonished at how little it had changed. I even ate the ooefy, fooey, cheesy *frittatina di pasta* for a second time. We visited the National Archeological Museum (which also has G-rated exhibits, thankfully), but I couldn't bring myself to visit the porn room with my kids. After all, wouldn't I be a horrible mother if I took my kids to see a room filled with sexually themed objects? The family visit was when I would indeed blush. The kids? They just giggled.

Lesson learned: If I ever return to Naples, I will memorize the lyrics to *O Sole Mio* and walk the streets singing it even though I can't sing.

Lesson not learned: Why am I not writing an entire book about Naples? Yes, it's that great.

Welcome to Paradise

The island of Capri is touristy and expensive. Food I couldn't afford. Souvenirs I didn't need. Overpriced Blue Grotto tour, during which I would have to wait 45 minutes until our boat could venture in to view the actual Blue Grotto (allegedly featuring really, *really* blue water). Said boat loaded with wealthy German tourists, to add to the indignity. Sorry, Germans, I wasn't wealthy.

But after I went, I wondered why the island, located approximately one hour off the coast of southern Italy, had the right to be as beautiful as it was.

There was no way I could afford to spend the night, but at least I could look around and walk up the steep sidewalks to the Monte Solaro chairlift. Taxi? Bahaha.

I was afraid of the chairlift at first. But when I saw people old enough to be my grandparents descending, I thought I could breathe deeply and avoid looking down. It was comparable to a ski lift, but I was not yet a skier. I did learn to do so many years later thanks to my husband's encouragement, and thankfully never ended up in traction as a result. As more than one person has said, "The problem with skiing is gravity."

Deep breath and let's go. As I ascended, I forgot that I was routinely lonely. I forgot that I couldn't converse in Italian to the point that I could make an actual acquaintance. I just looked at the view in astonishment. I spoke to a couple of English-speaking concession employees who actually lived on the island, and became green with envy. Of course, I didn't tell them that.

Returning to the mainland on the boat, some guy approached me and asked the usual questions: where ya from, where ya going. I told him I was returning to Germany and he asked, "Do you like Germany?" I responded, "No, not really." Right then, we remembered the boat was full of Germans and just busted up laughing. After we exchanged entirely too many German tourist jokes, he asked me on a date and said if I declined, he would kiss me right then…and he did. Right in front of God and everybody, including all the Germans, who were offended that we were actually having fun. The nerve of us!

Lesson not learned: I'll never understand why I did not immediately relocate to Capri while I was young and free.

Sicilian Born

It's a long haul to get to Sicily. I wanted to go there with my family in 2013, but it was hard. The only affordable flights were canceled regularly, and we really didn't want to chance that with a family of five. But I made it there when I was traveling on my own and tolerant of interminable train rides.

From Naples, it was an 11-hour—or, seemingly, 11-year—train ride. At that point in my travels, a ride of that duration was still an effort, but I wanted to see where my grandparents came from.

On the way to Palermo, I stopped off in Trabia. What a cute town; its population is probably the same as that of the town I currently live in. Is that my grandpa playing chess with a neighbor? Of course not, but the culture resonated.

As I strolled, I imagined my grandparents strolling these streets, then taking the opportunity to come to America when it presented itself. And they did. Heck, my paternal grandpa was literally --not figuratively--the first person listed on the Ellis Island log that documented his journey with other Italian immigrants. And he had a reasonable amount of money in his pocket compared to the other passengers. Definitely not rich, but enough to get a start after clearing Ellis Island customs. And I can only imagine how excited he was, being the first person in line and all.

I could easily picture my paternal grandma living there, although I barely knew her. Because she only spoke Italian and only wore demure black dresses, she scared seven-year-old me, even though Dad translated. But in Trabia, she would have totally fit in! And here in California, I've been told she sat outside the family property and brandished a shotgun to, um, "discourage" entitled passersby form picking and eating the cherries from the numerous trees during harvest season. Go badass grandma! (Full disclosure: I am a gun control advocate, but the visual for her resolve to defend her cherry trees is priceless.)

Even though Mom and Dad were born in America, they certainly embraced their Sicilian heritage. They even spoke in Italian when they didn't want us kids to know what they were talking about. I guess that's why Mom didn't want us to learn Italian. Parental confidentiality.

I've always wondered how Mom and Dad would have experienced Sicily had they made the journey. Mom wanted to travel, but Dad only left his hometown when we kids bought them anniversary trips to Las Vegas and Hawaii. How would they have reacted when they walked the streets their parents walked and spoke the language their parents spoke? I will never know because Dad lived a short drive minutes from his siblings and extended family. He was not me; he was content to hang out with his circle of family and longtime friends. Perhaps he agreed with the sentiment that "if you want all the comforts of home, you should stay there."

My parents and grandparents are buried in a cemetery reasonably nearby. Whenever I visit, I am astonished by how many of the dearly departed were born in tiny Trabia. Perhaps some relatives preceded them and somehow communicated how great

California was. Or there might have been an outbreak of disease. At any rate, my parents' cemetery could rightfully be characterized as "little Trabia." (BTW, I will skip the anecdote describing the creepy photo on my paternal grandma's grave. Ask my family if you know them, but I am not the only one who has noticed it.)

But enough with the possibly heartwarming sentiments of the dead and buried. Continuing on to Palermo, I was struck by how I took my life into my hands whenever I crossed a street. They didn't need no stinking traffic lights. For crissakes, pay attention, Toni! Apparently I hadn't learned anything in Naples.

The city's daytime street life was so animated. I was entertained by the manner in which street vendors featured whole fish caught from the sea, conveniently sliced into appropriate portions for their customers. They even used little microphones to hawk their catches in case their voices were not loud enough. *"Pesce fresco! Pesce fresco!"* Just in case passersby couldn't figure out they were selling super-fresh fish.

Time to eat. I availed myself of the fresh local fish, as well as a *mezzo-litro* of wine (half bottle, commonly ordered with meals) at a reasonably priced restaurant. When my waiter brought me a full bottle, I protested *"no, mezzo-litro!"* After my protest, he drew a little line in the bottle's condensation to indicate I should only drink to that level. And I abided, while simultaneously cracking up.

My two-star hotel was reasonably comfortable, but it curiously ran out of running water some afternoons. A hotel popular with honeymooners and I could not even be guaranteed a shower? But it was all good. The staff apologized. And I was in Sicily; I decided to shut up and deal with it.

Aside from the trauma of trying to cross a street, Palermo had a significant presence of organized crime. In order to cash a traveler's check (ask your elders) at a bank, I would have to pass through two alarmed doors and be permitted entry by staff in order to enter.

In addition, the nighttime streets were eerily quiet. In other Italian cities, the streets were teeming with people after dark, gabbing and enjoying each other. In Palermo, the only signs of life after dark were the clotheslines on apartment dwellers' balconies. That said, the city's crime rate is actually lower than that of other major Italian cities. Not sure if residents not venturing out after dark has anything to do with that.

Lesson learned: It was definitely worth the effort to walk the streets my grandparents walked.

Misery Business

After reviewing all the printed promotional material I received in snail mail, I planned to embark on New and Unfamiliar Experiences That Belonged on My Bucket List. Of course, travel is intended to be broadening and even educational at times. History was always my worst subject in high school, which I regret. But on my journey, I could visit great places and maybe even learn stuff.

That said, I was surprised at the number of supposedly great attractions and museums that amounted to two or three hours of my life I would never get back. On the other hand, I am thankful this chapter is shorter than the previous one.

"Cats" Is a (Painful) Memory

Because I had never been to a musical, it was time to get some culture in my life. Never mind that my limited wardrobe included nothing that was suitable for culture. Heck, I could go buy a dress and decent shoes; downtown Chicago is full of stores. On the other hand, no thanks. I'd already spent enough on the admission ticket.

I arrived at the downtown theatre and was excited. After all, "Cats" is one of the longest-running shows in musical theater history. Surely nobody would notice that I was dressed as if I were going on a hike. If they did, they apparently gossiped among themselves rather than giving me dismissively dirty looks. Go Chicago!

Curtain rises. One song, meh. Two songs, meh. I quickly realized this show was stupid. A guy in a lion suit twirling his tail as he sang? Really? At least "Memory" was a good song.

I left at intermission. I was probably missing a new episode of a bad TV show or a reasonably exciting baseball game. At least I could be assured that nobody would be wearing a lion suit and would definitely not sing stupid songs.

Lesson learned: In the words of PT Barnum, "Nobody ever went broke underestimating the intelligence of the American public."

I Wanna Rock, But Yawn

I can spontaneously remember three songs that theoretically evoke Stonehenge.

Spinal Tap's song ("Stonehenge") made this destination sound exciting and mysterious, although its performance in "This Is Spinal Tap" is nothing short of hilarious. Twisted Sister's song ("I Wanna Rock") just exacerbated the problem; it made me think I wanted to rock, but only at Stonehenge. After SpongeBob SquarePants spoofed "I Wanna Rock," I ended up doing a figurative Goofy Goober dance. I am allowed to crack myself up occasionally, but YouTube is your friend if you don't get the joke.

In a possible foreshadowing of how the day was to unfold, the British Rail clerk had to arrogantly correct my pronunciation of Salisbury: "*Solz-burry*, not *Sals-berry.*" Well, excuse the crap out of me.

Stonehenge was boring. Okay, I departed the tour bus and dutifully observed it. Wow, giant rocks. Woohoo.

I fully acknowledge that had I paid more attention in high school, or perhaps did some pre-travel research, I may have appreciated what a Serious and Impressive Place this is. However, I took a look, returned to the tour bus, and gabbed with the bus driver until we were done. Pee-Wee Herman's quote resonated in my mind: "But why? What's the significance? I don't know!"

Lesson learned: Some historical sites are diamonds, some historical sites are (actual) rocks. Sorry about that, Tom Petty; your actual lyrics are better than my attempts at deadpan humor. And I hope Gone Gator Music's team hasn't spotted this lyrics reference. I didn't mean it, and please don't make me pay for the rights to cite it.

The Town, Not the Bread

No idea why I wanted to go to Rye, UK; damn you, alluring tourist brochures. Perhaps I clung to the slim hope that I would run into Paul McCartney, who has an expansive ranch in East Sussex. Honestly, I don't know.

Arrived at the train station hungry. There was a pub near the station, and I quickly learned that pubs are not bars; they are "public houses." In other words, a welcoming place to have lunch without feeling compelled to have an alcoholic drink to accompany it.

The marquee item on the menu was a "Ploughman's Lunch." I knew I was not a ploughman (whatever that is), but it sounded local and authentic. Yes, please.

But it was semi-glorified bread and cheese, with a few other accompaniments such as pickled onions. Filled me up, which was the main goal. But the next time I have bread and cheese at home, I will refer to it as a "Ploughman's Snack." Gosh, I crack myself up sometimes.

Rye was as cute as a bug's ear, but there was nothing to do. Perhaps if I had read the tourist brochures more closely, I would have been more prepared. Or perhaps it was one of the places that required a car in order to see any of the great stuff. And I was fully unprepared to drive a car on the wrong side of the road. Too weird.

I was so bored that I got a second set of ear piercings just to kill time. Sorry I didn't run into you, Paul.

Lesson learned: Now I know what a Ploughman's Lunch is. Not sure how I survived without that fun fact.

I Still Haven't Found What I'm Looking For

Comparable to Barack Obama's 2008 comment about Hillary Clinton, Dublin is "likable enough."

Irish breakfasts are amazing. At home, a bowl of cornflakes is breakfast. In Ireland, we're just getting started. The free breakfast at my room was so over-the-top that I barely ate the rest of the day.

The only reasonably memorable outing in Dublin was the Guinness brewery tour. I've already established that I don't love beer, but love factory tours.

The tour was not nearly as stinky as the Anheuser-Busch brewery in St. Louis (refer to "Yeah, This is Better Than Working"). The final treat for the tour participants was, what else, free beer in the tasting room. Of course, I had to partake even though I don't like beer and had probably drunk two in my life. I was sure it would taste better if I was at the site at which it was brewed.

Ewww.

Even though Dublin was likable enough, couldn't I at least have run into a member of the Irish band U2? I would have settled for The Edge, although TBD if I would recognize anyone other than Bono.

Lesson learned: I could like a town if it served breakfasts as bountiful as I experienced in Dublin. Yes, sometimes my appetite takes precedence.

I'll Hit You Baby, One More Time

I felt I had to go to Oktoberfest. I was in Munich, it was happening, and it was supposed to be a good time. Never mind that I don't drink beer, so it was comparable to a vegetarian going to a Kansas City barbecue event.

Upon entering the air-quote "festival," I saw grown men wearing lederhosen and grown women wearing dirndls. Okay, everyone can honor their heritage, but the children compelled to wear the same attire were probably hoping they didn't run into their friends. The teenagers probably told their parents, "Are you kidding me?" In German, of course.

Oktoberfest was rather traditional, not a par-tay as I would expect after attending American festivals that involved beer. Traditional food, I guess. Traditional music, I guess. I was bored and hoped the air-quote "traditional food" would somehow settle in my tummy without making me vomit.

The Germans at Oktoberfest are fine; they can handle their alcohol and, IMO, really didn't drink that much. Their fest is about heritage, lederhosen, and peasant dresses, not about Jell-O shots. They were also rocking the bumper cars. In that respect, go locals! Of course, however, someone seeking to be my Bad Boyfriend (or hour-long tryst) found me. Let the boorishness begin.

I was seated, trying-trying-trying to enjoy the music. No Tom Petty covers? Heck, the Heartbreakers were on Rockpalast (West Germany's answer to Ed Sullivan and American Bandstand, only better). Couldn't a band at least cover "American Girl?" Apparently not.

While I waited for an actual good song, a drunken British guy approached me. I was just doing my usual happy and dismissive talk, but then he started making some awful and insulting remarks.

"It appears that you're a prostitute. Judging from your clothes, you walk the streets. Whaddaya say...shall we?" (Not exact words, but close enough.) I serenely walked away, leaving the Brit to his beer and his own devices.

LOL, not really.

I gave him some filthy, filthy looks and he still didn't back off. I started punching him—five or six or seven times according to my journal. At that point, people were starting to stare, but hopefully not placing wagers on the outcome.

Geez, it's not like I was wearing a thong and a sparkly top. I was just a young woman trying to see the world and was probably wearing sweat pants and a possibly amusing T-shirt. Again, beer is yucky and I was sober as a judge. It was unclear why anyone would think I was there to look for, um, clients. How was I conveying that

I was desperately searching for a sugar daddy that would permit me to put an end to my iffy life on the streets? Stupid Brit, you don't know me. I earned the money in my pocket from an actual job, not from performing sex acts on pathetic jerks such as you. I had been issued a business card with a title and everything. Take that!

I knew security guards were nearby, so I subsequently launched a loud F-bomb and walked away. Shortly thereafter, I encountered a couple of Sardinian men who were nice enough, but I saw where it was heading. Exit, stage left.

I will never understand why I attracted so many men who assumed that even if I was not a prostitute, I was quite possibly a slut. Geez, the only time I wore semi-revealing clothes is when it was hotter than you-know-where. Definitely not a Kardashian. Heck, my acne hadn't even cleared up yet.

Lesson learned: Oktoberfest is overrated. Dumb. Perhaps if I had been wearing traditional German attire, I would have had a better experience. But I would never wear a dirndl. I have my dignity.

My Bologna

Somehow I ended up in Bologna, Italy. Perhaps the train schedule was convenient and I would be able to have a power nap during the trip.

My initial impression of Bologna was good, although I was surprised that my backpack was searched before I could board the train en route. The reason was that the city suffered a terrorist bombing at their train station—referred to as the Bologna Massacre—in 1980, during which 85 people were killed and 200 were wounded. Five years later and they were still checking backpacks. Go them!

Bologna is known alternatively as the "Fat City" for its food, the "Red City" for its leftie politics, or the "Learned City" because its university is the oldest in the world. Its most impressive aspect, however, was that the city's architects created shaded sidewalks. Wait, what?

Italy is gosh-darn hot in summer. However, the walkways throughout the central city were nicely shaded, and I didn't have to drown in sweat while sightseeing. The city has some beautiful churches and other attractions, but I remember the shade. Trust me, it was a surprising and welcome relief.

Furthermore, the city was not overrun with tourists. People were patient with foreigners, and my *poco Italiano* wasn't awful. I assume the breakfast joints were pleased that they weren't deluged with entitled Americans seeking bacon and eggs, as apparently the Florence restaurants were. Read on.

I did have pasta with Bolognese sauce, and I guess it was good. But I didn't really know what to do in town aside from eat, then repel amorous men, both of which I regularly did throughout Italy. (BTW, the Spanish were worse and the Sicilians were gentlemen.) I guess I could have done more research, but once, again I have no idea how I ended up there.

Lesson learned: Bologna is great place to live, but I wouldn't want to visit.

We Have a Winner

I really don't intend to pick on places people love…except for Nebraska. Joke: Why do people take an instant dislike to Nebraska? Because it saves time. Sorry, let's move on.

One morning, the bus dropped me off in Williamsburg, Virginia, at 5 AM. The station didn't open until 7:30. Forced to play bridge troll, I yanked out my sleeping bag and slept on a bench until the sun came up. Thankfully, that was the only time I had to do that.

According to my glossy tourist brochures, Colonial Williamsburg was a very popular place, so let's do it. However, this alleged "attraction" wins the award for the stupidest place I've ever visited. Sigh, I could have been in a more entertaining city. Or even at work, for crissakes. But no, Williamsburg. Thanks for nothing, tourist brochures.

The alleged fun begins. Wow, this lady in a historically accurate dress is weaving. Wow, this man in historically accurate male apparel is creating something that should interest me. I could sympathize with the children, who were undoubtedly thinking, "Mom and Dad, can we please just go to Disney World, ride a frightening roller coaster, and eat junk food? Can't we just learn this stuff in school?" Believe me, I felt their pain.

I left in boredom and disgust, then attempted to sell the remainder of my multi-day ticket (multi-day, really?) to another family. I was a sweet and reasonably innocent tourist, trying to convince others I simply was unable to stay for another day because I had to get back home to my ailing mother…not because Colonial Williamsburg was stupid.

Most people I approached treated me as if I were a scalper trying to pawn off fake concert tickets outside a major venue. I mean, come on; my mother was sick!

I ultimately did sell the ticket at a loss, but at least I was able to escape the historical lameness and move on to somewhere that didn't stink. Or, at least, get an actual hotel room that wasn't awful.

Lesson learned: I am not a historical reenactment woman. Although I regularly attempted to move out of my comfort zone, sometimes it wasn't comfortable.

PART THREE

Bongiorno Lenny!
ITALY IS THE GREATEST! Honestly, the people here really
know how to live; everything is so relaxed. Italians are so nice and
helpful. I've even picked up some Italian.
It will break my heart to leave this beautiful place…"la dolce vita"
indeed!

--Postcard to Lenny, August 10, 1985 (yes, he saved all 14 of them)

Show Me the Money

At the tender age of 18, I stumbled into a mundane cashier job that turned out be a blast. It also played a moderate role in financing my travels.

It was a job at a car wash, but not one primarily staffed by ex-convicts. No, it was upscale! Cute theme park locations, the flagship of which was a replica of a Mississippi River paddleboat. I will not name the car wash, but they strived to be the place where owners of really pricey cars could patronize without worrying about their hubcaps being stolen during the process. And heck, customers could even buy a bottle of wine or (I kid you not) a diamond necklace in its gift shop before reclaiming their squeaky clean car. The owner's wife and mother-in-law apparently needed a way to occupy their time and stay out of his way. I assume his exasperated response was, "Okay, you ladies can manage the gift shop."

The owner decided it would be a brilliant idea to franchise the concept, and for quite a while it was great. I was the person chosen to travel to franchisees' locations to train the cashier staff about how to use our latest, greatest, up-to-datest cash registers. This may sound odd, but the technology was very cutting-edge at the time. Data communications…it was like magic. Modems big enough that an actual, breathing mouse could move in and disable it (yes, this really happened). In hindsight, I can just picture my boss Pat protesting at executive-level meetings. "Why are we doing this? Can't the locations simply call us on the phone with their numbers? We can skip all the techno bells and whistles, then use the ginormous modems to send them their gee-whiz performance reports using the ginormous modems. As long as a mouse doesn't take up residence."

It was my job to make this cutting-edge system work, and I mostly did. I even got an overstated title and a business card. 20 years old and a business card? Who knew?

I apparently developed a reputation for being rather good at my job. Because of that, I was able to intersperse occasional work days, "advise" locations about how to "improve their operations," get paid under the table, and receive a free hotel room. Never would I decline a free hotel room and a couple of days' cash pay. Especially when it would enable me to travel to places I really wanted to visit.

My coworkers were quite the motley crew, and I could probably write another book about them. There was at least one confirmed convict and probably others who have since joined the convict club. But we won't go there.

Vending Machine Dinner

There are allegedly songs about Dallas, but I just can't.

Although I had been there previously, I agreed to do another brief stint, which had four car washes. I only worked at one, but that was enough.

The joke (but not really) was that one of the locations was in such a wealthy area that the actual car owners were Too Important to get their own cars washed; it was their staff's job. Okay, rich people, stay home and count your money.

The owner, Chris, was a wealthy man. His (presumably) trophy wife was, of course, blonde. I think all wives of wealthy Texans were required to be blonde in that era, but perhaps that's just me.

I performed my usual task—kindly telling the cashier staff what they were doing wrong—but at the end of the day, they drove me back to my hotel with a see-you-in-the-morning sendoff. No car, and absolutely nowhere to eat. I was reduced to eating vending machine junk food.

I didn't expect to have a night on the town, but someone could have included a dinner stop in the ride back to my good-enough hotel. Perhaps a fast-food drive-in. Convenience store. Anything other than chips and candy bars. And was it okay if I starved if I didn't happen to have exact change?

The good news was that I didn't have to run into another (almost) Bad Boyfriend. I had spoken to Terry on the phone several times. Charming guy, but he was arrested for embezzlement. Yet another loser.

Lesson learned: Happiness was Dallas in my rear-view mirror.

Yes, I Hurt Myself

Another serendipitous outing as a result of my job. I loved being able to kindly tell people what they were doing wrong.

The Houston crew treated me very well. As it turned out, another startup was happening during my trip. Hooray, I was able to make a few bucks and get a free two-star hotel room.

Rather than being driven to my hotel and being wished luck regarding my vending machine dinner, I was able to have dinner with my kinda-sorta colleagues at a restaurant in Galveston that was suitably named Crazy Cajun. Their marketing slogan: "Gonna make you hurt yo'self."

I soon found out the significance of the slogan. While we waited for our entrees, we received *amuse-bouches,* which are greatly glorified appetizers. Wow! This is great! Until I adventurously tried a raw oyster...thank God I didn't vomit at the table. I came *this* close.

I ate so much that night that I probably didn't eat for two days (okay, exaggerating). OMG, Cajun food! Crawfish! Jambalaya! Stuff I'd never eaten before! By the end of the night, yeah...I hurt myself. Crazy Cajun wasn't kidding.

It was so pleasant to spend time with people I would not otherwise hang out with. Texas was weird for me because the ladies were married, while I was barely dating. The guys were a blast, but no romantic interest. Just eat, laugh, and eat some more. And more. And more.

Lessons learned:

- Need to wear stretchy pants for such a night of gluttony.
- Food can be gosh-darn great.
- No raw oysters. Have fun with that.

Hangout With a Dad

I had a one-day, um, consultation gig with the Milburn, New Jersey, car wash. I stayed with my car wash friend Joyce. After I finished my one day of paid employment, she had to work. Her dad volunteered to entertain me in New York City for the afternoon. I soon discovered that dads can be fun.

We drove into the city. During that era, needy men would wash windshields at a stoplight and expect to be paid. However, because her dad would have none of this, he yelled at the guys to get the heck away from his car. Which they did. No idea how he managed to pull that off; he was such a kind and benign guy.

After we parked, I honestly don't recall what we did. But the knish! I had never had one before, but we got them from a hole in the wall located downstairs from somewhere in Manhattan. Why did it take me twentysomething years to try one? Oh yeah, I'm a Sicilian from California; we always ate pasta.

When we returned to their home, he sweetly said to his wife, "Honey, we need to go to the city more often."

Must give a shoutout to Joyce. We went to a Tom Petty concert. I enjoyed it, even though that was my least favorite tour. I am, however, sorry we lost touch and hope her life is going well.

Lesson learned: I could have fun with anyone if each of us had the same sense of adventure. I hope Joyce's dad is still with us.

Hangout With Another Dad

Who thinks of Alabama as a destination for a post-college trip? Me, apparently. However, I did have my reasons. Their car wash had a franchise in Vestavia, a wealthy suburb of Birmingham, and the owners liked me. I had three paid under-the-table workdays. They even let me use one of their cars. Not smart.

It was a mundane gig. Once again, my job was to train cashiers and to tell them what they were doing wrong. I was accustomed to the drill, but it was always pleasant to meet the motley crews. One of the workers was nicknamed "Frog" because he could voice a plausible frog-like sound. No, I never knew anyone who could do that.

As far as I could tell, none of the employees were criminals. Refreshing change of pace. A cashier's husband was indeed a criminal, but let's not go there.

Robert and Dick were brothers and the owners of two franchise locations. They booked me a hotel that was not awful and gave me the use of a really nice car. They even supplied me with a pile of free meal coupons for a couple of Tennessee-based franchises. How did I thank them? Sigh.

I filled up the car's gas tank and stupidly drove off without before removing the nozzle from the tank. After I destroyed said nozzle, I was mortified and also astonished that they still paid me for my work. But this next memory is fun.

Dick was old enough to be my dad and offered to show me the sights. Our first stop was at the late, great Uncle Mort's, a Culinary Hall of Fame honoree located in the rural town of Jasper. I ordered catfish, which I had eaten many times. They served it with sorghum syrup, whatever that was.

What could go wrong? I would find out shortly.

When my catfish arrived, it had a face and was looking at me. Eww eww eww! I realized I had previously only eaten catfish filets, not catfish corpses. I managed to eat it, but avoided eye contact to avoid answering his question, "What have I done to deserve this?" After I guiltily consumed him, I decided to name him Paul.

After lunch, Dick and I returned to Vestavia and pleasantly wandered around town. As we wandered, we encountered a church at which a wedding was in progress. Impulsively, we crashed it. When we did so, one of the parents' heads exploded because we were dressed so casually. We left, then collapsed into laughter. No, we didn't crash the reception.

Lessons learned:

- Once again, father figures can be a blast.
- If and when I ordered catfish, make sure it's a filet. Paul's pathetic fishy face still occasionally haunts me in my dreams, and I do apologize to the poor guy. I have since become a vegetarian, and I hope Paul feels better to know I wouldn't eat his grandson while he stares at me plaintively.

Are You Ready to Rumble After a Stroll on a Gorgeous Beach?

Pensacola, Florida, due to another working vacation gig. It consisted of the usual couple of days telling their cashiers what they were doing wrong, but my hotel was much, much nicer than the one in Vestavia. No car, but it didn't matter. I was comfortable and was walking distance from the white sand beach.

Until then, I didn't even know white sand beaches existed. And the sand was sooo soft...like walking on a giant expanse of baking powder. Possibly another best-kept regional secret, but perhaps California didn't want to get the word out about the gorgeous Florida beaches. On the other hand, there are no hurricanes in California and it doesn't rain in summer. Call it a draw?

Unlike Vestavia, I don't remember many of the employees I worked with, the exception of which was TJ, who took me on a kinda-sorta-but-not-really date to a WWF type of wrestling match. Pretend wrestling.

This was not a first-time experience for me because Dad loved Big Time Wrestling (the precursor to WWF), and I watched the fake matches every Saturday afternoon as a child. No screen time limits; Mom was probably happy to be left the heck alone.

But back to Pensacola.

TJ was not my type, but was sweet in a redneck way. I enjoyed the over-the-top pretend wrestling and the over-the-top dorky costumes, makeup, and alleged hairstyles. And TJ was really quite the gentleman.

As it turned out, I was in Pensacola on the day of the 1986 All-Star Game, which showcases the best performers of the first half of the year's baseball season. I had the pleasure of watching the now semi-disgraced Roger Clemens strike out the side in the first inning. Lounging on a pretty bed. Eating an unremarkable dinner. Sleeping comfortably for free. Not awful.

Lessons learned:

- Some baseball memories inexplicably stuck with me. I have come to realize that many, many games are boring, but the great ones always resonate. Roger Clemens was awesome, and it was an amazing year for him. The controversies had not yet surfaced.

- Even though TJ was not my type, we had a good time. Because he bought me a good-enough dinner at the venue, my tummy was happy when I returned to my hotel. For at least one of my other work-related trips, I had been dropped off at my hotel room even though I was reduced to vending machines for sustenance. Dallas, I am talking to you.

Pat, You Were a Great Boss, But I'm Not Shot Out

In hindsight, it is interesting that I semi-regularly hung out with dad-like figures. It is also baffling at how fun it was.

Pat, my car wash boss (I was still on leave at the time but had not resigned) and some of the other higher-ups had come to New Orleans for a convention. Somehow we made our plans without smartphones. But okay, let's have an evening.

Not many people agree to meet up with their boss and other Responsible Adults on Bourbon Street. To be fair, Pat wasn't old enough to be my dad, but he had a wife. Kids. Concepts that were foreign to me. Heck, I wasn't even out of the ramen-for-dinner phase of my life.

Although Pat taught me so much and treated me as a competent adult, he made it clear who was the boss. We regularly did car wash franchise openings in many states. When we were preparing for a franchise opening and I said "I didn't have time" to perform a task he requested, he had a deadpan response: "Wanna walk to El Paso?" Conversation over and I did whatever he needed me to do.

However, we somehow managed to arrange a meetup at the 544 Club (now called the Funky 544…good grief). As worlds collided, The Wives had spent the afternoon shopping on Royal Street, an unreasonably pricey street I could never afford even now. On the other hand, I don't need stuff. No interest, but no judgment either. Wives, you be you.

As The Wives shopped, I was visiting my fast friends on Bourbon Street. Because I visited so many times, I had gotten to know a few of the barkers who tried to beckon tourists into their clubs. Chris, I think I saw you in 2014, but after 29 years, who knows? I probably should have approached you, but didn't.

Time for the alleged "club," which consisted of reasonably adequate music and unreasonably priced drinks. We listened to the tourist jazz, rock, and whatever else. During the show, Pat bought me a shot of something (which I probably couldn't afford on my budget) and insisted I down it. I did.

His response? "I have always appreciated that you always do what I tell you to do." The Irish Catholic he was, he certainly had the gift of gab. RIP, Pat.

Lesson learned: Pat was the best boss I ever had, and I occasionally quote him to this day. In 1988, he told me I was "shot out." But he was probably envious that I had waaay more fun than he ever did.

There's Always Someone Cooler Than You

I gotta write about my dear friend Charlie, who is my friend to this day. Sometimes years go by without us talking, but we always pick up where we left off.

We met at a car wash opening in San Antonio, and gosh was he a Boy Scout, and was so different from the people I was accustomed to hanging out with: Bad Boyfriends, future inmates.

In addition to seeing a Texas Rangers game in Arlington, we hung out in downtown Dallas for a day or so. We spent the day gabbing and visiting some strange museums. A telephone museum, for crissakes! Geez, we should have visited Dealey Plaza or the Texas School Book Depository. Regardless, it was great to catch up.

He is one of the best friends I've ever had, and shepherded me through an awful time in my life. In 2014, he traveled from Texas to attend my daughter's wedding, which truly touched me.

Lesson learned: Lifelong friendships are a gift and are worth nurturing. Charlie, you rock so much that I was willing to spend time in Texas to hang out with you.

Hanging in the Gallery

Virtually all of the great art galleries are in Italy. I tried, really I did, to summon memories of great galleries in our nation. I probably could have included the New York City and San Francisco Museums of Modern Art. But Italy…what deal did they make with the devil? Anybody? Anybody? At least I included a couple of galleries which are indeed located in our great nation.

That said, the violence in religious art was a recurrent theme. I thought thou shalt not kill.

Don't get me wrong; I am grateful I was able to see so many Great Works of Art. Michelangelo's "Pieta" is probably the greatest statue of all time. Viewing his works was itself worth the price of an across-the-pond plane ticket. See, I'm not that jaded.

However, why the violent depictions of saints' martyred deaths? Of course I understand that the artists wanted to convey the suffering that faithful followers were willing to endure in the name of their Lord. Their fates were undeniably awful, but did it need to be so graphic? Are these art museums or slasher movies?

And then there are the depictions of Our Father, Who Art in Heaven. I completely get that too; according to the Old Testament, we need to have a healthy fear of Our Father. Poor Job (read the Book of Job or watch "It's a Wonderful Life"). But gosh, God is Our Father, not a gang member. Any possibility to tone it down? I get it already! I'll repent!

Some of the paintings grossed out 22-year-old me. Some of them still gross out 60-year-old me. But what was the point? Would I want to follow these saints into martyrdom? Yeah, right; I could do that (not). Pretty sure I can continue to feed the hungry and clothe the naked to the best of my ability. Please drop the bows, arrows, and stones.

On a lighter note, I loved the ginormous paintings that depicted an unknown random guy addressing a sizable crowd. If you look and look and look, there are always a couple of attendees in the painted crowd who are rolling their eyes or dozing off. I love reality.

But gosh, didn't women paint back then? Or were they too busy preparing the nightly gruel to feed their families? Raising their sons (not many daughters) to face martyrdom? Telling their husbands to take it down a notch and to please remember to bring home the missing gruel ingredients from the sidewalk vendor?

And gosh again, couldn't these artists have painted a still life on occasion, or even Campbell's Soup cans? Okay, the latter had not been invented yet, but the former certainly existed.

But let's move on. Indulge me in my sighing and occasional crying after seeing so much great art.

Dead Presidents (Except for Five)

Honestly, I'm not trying to audition as a tourism writer. That said, the National Portrait Gallery in Washington, DC, is my second favorite place on the planet. Not sure what #1 is.

The 17 Smithsonian museums in DC are consistently awesome. In particular, the Air and Space Museum is fourth on the list of most-visited museums in our nation. (In fairly recent years, I remember telling one of my kids a dumb joke during our tour, but you had to be there.) As a bonus, they are all free. Go Smithsonian!

However, the National Portrait Gallery is in a class by itself. It is one of the more benign—that is, less crowded--Smithsonian museums. As an added bonus, it is located in an area that actually features intermittent shade, unlike the blazing hot National Mall. I'm happy that it is not as crowded as the others, but sad that many do not recognize it as the treasure it is.

I can rarely last more than two hours in any gallery or museum. However, I have easily spent three hours at the Gallery during at least a half-dozen visits over the years. Every time I make it to DC, I go there. Unfortunately, it's been fourteen years. Sigh.

The Gallery honors many notable American writers, athletes, activists, and a few performers (no Kardashians allowed, thank God). However, the Hall of Presidents is its marquee attraction; it displays the official portraits of our previous 44 presidents. Those who wrote the portraits' accompanying fun-fact descriptions were geniuses because they managed to convey the humanity of each of them. Yes, I know we are at #45 (because of the Prior Guy), but I haven't been there since his official portrait was unveiled. If someone could convey the humanity of #45, wow. And #46's portrait will not be unveiled until he leaves office...in case you don't know how official presidential portraits work.

Whenever I visit, I feel like I just had coffee with George Washington, Franklin Roosevelt, and maybe even Richard Nixon, among others. FDR's portrait is simply astonishing even if you are a Republican.

But William Henry Harrison, what the heck? He didn't need no stinking warm clothes. On March 4, 1841, he gave the longest inaugural speech in history without a hat, gloves, or coat. Sometime later that month, he went for a stroll while similarly underdressed. He ultimately contracted pneumonia and was gone only 31 days after he became president. Because the Secret Service was not established until 1865, there were no scolds insisting he put on some winter gear, for crissakes. Or stay in his residence until the weather wasn't awful.

Lesson learned: If I ever thought government couldn't get anything right, the Hall of Presidents disabused me of that notion. I never get tired of it, and I loved the assurance that the previous leaders of the free world put their pants on one leg at a time, just as we all do. Hoping that in the foreseeable future, the leader of the free world will wear a festive evening gown for the celebratory inaugural ball.

96 Tears

The Art Institute of Chicago is the World Series of art in our nation.

Norman Effing Rockwell (thanks, Lana Del Rey)! Vincent Effing Van Gogh! American Effing Gothic! Effing Nighthawks!

Marc Effing Chagall! I slightly teared up upon viewing all of these artists' works, but Rockwell? Pass the tissues, please, as I was bawling like a baby. And his triple self-portrait…had anybody else thought of this?

Rockwell is so mischaracterized. Kids (and even contemporaries), he was primarily known for his covers of the Saturday Evening Post, in which he painted heartwarming images depicting heartwarming White American families. But wait, there's more.

As he progressed in his art, and after he left the Post, he painted something truly moving: "The Problem We All Live With," which depicted a young Ruby Bridges when she attended a newly desegregated New Orleans elementary school. Not exactly a heartwarming Post cover of a mythical nuclear family enjoying Thanksgiving dinner.

Her innocence, contrasted with the stains of tomatoes thrown on the school's walls, was conveyed brilliantly. I had the privilege of seeing this portrait at a traveling exhibit, but OMG, it is so worth it to see it if you're anywhere near his museum in Massachusetts. His triple self-portrait is also at that museum, so go there. Even in the dead of winter.

Lesson learned: Sometimes iconic artists are oversimplified (Rockwell, I'm talking to you), but after seeing their works in person, it was worth it to take the time to research a bit more about them.

Lesson not learned: Why didn't I learn to paint?

Okay, Just Tell Me Which Paintings I Should Like

Madrid's Museo del Prado was allegedly one of the World's Greatest Museums, but I was bored. My shins were giving me grief, which didn't help my mood and tourist enthusiasm. I will spare you the random "OMG my legs hurt" journal entries, but my visit to the Prado was comically painful.

Attempting to be a trooper, I purchased my ticket. After entering, however, I realized it was an exercise in futility. For one thing, the pain; for another, I didn't really care about the artwork.

Fra Angelico, I know I'm supposed to be impressed. Peter Paul Rubens, ditto. Rembrandt, you're just a guy, but perhaps there will be a band named after you someday. (Spoiler alert: There was, and they sang the "Friends" theme song. Please tell me the band's name wasn't inspired by his painting titled "The Anatomy Lesson of Dr. Nicolaes Tulp.")

After, um, "enjoying" the Prado, my shins were starting to seriously hurt. I actually thought I would have to cut my trip short. I had been doing a lot of walking throughout my travels, but suddenly my shins protested, "*No mas!*" (Only God knows how they learned to speak Spanish.) Part of me wondered if this is what it felt like to be 60. Well, now being 60, I know. Yeah, this is what it feels like.

Although I spoke enough Spanish to be dangerous, I couldn't picture going to a doctor, pointing to my shins, and groaning "owww!" Instead, I went to a *farmacia* (pharmacy), at which I pointed to my shins and groaned "owww!" What was the remedy? *Aspirina.* Aspirin, for crissakes. I bought some, took it back to my zero-star room, and was good enough after a couple of days of rest.

I did give the Prado another chance and was able to focus on the artwork I personally liked, not the ones the so-called experts told me I should like. That made it better. Even so, I recently thumbed through the "Visitor's Guide to the Prado" in my scrapbook. After thumbing through it, I understand why I was bored.

Apparently there was a certain artistic period during which everyone's portraits looked largely alike. What was that about—laziness? Even though all squirrels look alike in my neighborhood, was there ever a time during which all people looked alike?

Thankfully, I was able to salvage my time in the city. I was even able to talk to actual Spaniards in actual Spanish. Who knew? Some random men (are there any others at this point in my travels?) invited me to join them for flamenco dancing later that night, but at that point, I was thankful I could walk.

Lesson learned: I could view great artists' works and make up my own stories about their lives and motivations. Rembrandt's wife was not exactly a Kardashian…maybe he needed the distraction of painting? I could enjoy his art while simultaneously cracking myself up.

Michelangelo and Raphael…No, Not the Ninja Turtles

If at all possible, please avoid Italy in the summertime. So hot. Tourist attractions so crowded. Only God know why I decided to go in July. It's not like I had to worry about school; I had graduated college. But again, I was 22; I wasn't thinking.

Although the Vatican Museums are a royal pain because of the summertime crowds, the artwork is undeniably worth the effort. The crying began in the Sistine Chapel; it continued in the Raphael rooms.

Michelangelo was 61 years old when he began painting a 42x39-foot ceiling in the chapel for the next five years. I am his age, and it's a good day when I can ascend my home's staircase.

Raphael was the diminutive of his actual name: Raffaelo Sanzino or Raffaelo Santi, depending on your source. Regardless, he did some crazy-good paintings until he passed at age 37. One can only imagine what he could have done if he lived longer.

I did love the Vatican museums, but honestly, it was hot and sweaty and crowded. Thankfully, my mood greatly improved when I went to the gelato joint near the museum. Long lines, but it didn't matter. For once, the guidebooks got it right by characterizing its gelato as one of the best in Rome. While I patiently waited for my fix, I amused myself by watching the nuns with backpacks. Wait, what?

In our great nation, you rarely see nuns in their traditional gear ("habits") these days. However, they were ubiquitous in Italy. Imagine a pious woman dressed in a pious outfit...with a backpack. Funny and impressive, but I felt intrusive about photographing the badass nuns. That said, they are forever etched in my brain.

Lessons learned:

- Either avoid Italy in summer or wear as few clothes as possible.
- Michelangelo was a genius, as was Raphael.

Can't Take My Eyes Off You

Pretty certain no American musician has ever written a song about Florence, Italy, not even Tom Petty. I had to attempt a clever title on my own for this vignette. And may or may not have failed.

I know I tend to complain about supposedly great tourist attractions (I love being cynical). But the Uffizi just blew me away. And the rumor among the crowd was that Henry Kissinger was in attendance. Who knew someone could plot a war crime in a world class art museum?

Michelangelo's "The Creation of Adam" was amazing. Botticelli's "The Birth of Venus" was just a few feet away. Gasps. Repeated gasps.

Elsewhere in Florence, I'm glad I saw the statue of David, but I remain convinced it was moved to the Accademia Gallery to ensure tourists would pay yet another admission price in order to view The Great Statue with their own eyes. David, woohoo! Rest of exhibit, yawn.

It was picturesque to see the city wake up…residents, not tourists. I probably witnessed this because I arrived on an early train, but I saw a collection of Renaissance-ish statues in a beautiful plaza. The sun had not risen, so they were illuminated by spotlights. Pulled out my camera, and of course…right when I was ready to capture the picture, the spotlights dimmed and the sun came out. I was and still am a horrible photographer, but the scene is forever captured in my mind's eye.

Lesson learned: Even if I'd seen the greatest works of art in a book, online, or in a documentary, seeing them with my own eyes was a seminal experience. And I might have run into Henry Kissinger. Not sure if that would have been a good thing.

Houses of the Holy

As I have already established, I am a practicing Catholic and am always trying to get better at it. For that reason, I made a mostly successful effort to attend Mass whenever I could. Same script, same gymnastics (stand, sit, kneel, repeat), but the subtle local differences were fascinating.

Aside from the salvation thing, my affection for Catholicism grew when in 2017, Pope Francis invoked a Tom Petty lyric when he advocated for refugees: "Even if they are refugees, they don't have to live like them," at least, where education is an issue.

To quote Winston Churchill, "Catholicism is the worst religion, except for all the others." You don't have to be Catholic to enjoy these anecdotes, and I promise not to preach. Although if you don't acknowledge Catholicism as the One True Church, you will burn in hell.

Haha, gotcha.

I Had a Friend Who Appalled Some Narrow-Minded People

I met Champ (hopefully his parents didn't really name him that) because he was an unhoused man in New Orleans hanging out at the Moon Walk. I love the Moon Walk, a promenade on the shores of the Mississippi River at the edge of the French Quarter, but it was a bit of a magnet to the unhoused in addition to wealthy tourists. Speaking for myself, my ritual was to eat jambalaya (sooo yummy) on its rock-laden shoreline as soon as I arrived in town.

After Champ and I spent a few minutes gabbing, I had to go to Mass. I invited him to join me at the St. Louis Cathedral, a two-minute walk from our bench. He dutifully left his beer outside the cathedral and actually listened pretty closely to the priest's homily, a talk which theoretically should give guidance as to how the day's readings (which consisted of Bible excerpts) should spur you into action to live a better life. At several points, Champ would exclaim, "I hear you, bro," which resulted in more than one dirty look.

Really? Didn't my Lord come to serve us all? Didn't Jesus hang out with prostitutes and tax collectors? After Mass, Champ retrieved his beer and we parted ways. I can't make this stuff up.

Lesson learned: It was a gift to take a random person to Mass; I can only hope Champ attended Mass on his own after I continued my travels. But I don't think Jesus would be pleased with the people who gave him dirty looks.

"Wanna See the Crypt?"

Fast forward to 2012. As I had previously experienced when I visited Philadelphia on my own (refer to "The Wrong Thing to Do"), summer was horribly hot. Thankfully, my husband and I could afford a hotel with much-needed air conditioning for us and our kids. Go us!

After making fools of ourselves at the ginormous fountain on the renowned Benjamin Franklin Parkway (you had to be there), we were able to tour the Basilica of Saints Peter and Paul, located a couple of blocks away. In case you don't know, a Basilica is a Catholic church given special privileges by the Vatican because it is especially holy. Yes, I'm oversimplifying.

Because anti-Catholicism was not uncommon at the time of its construction, the Basilica's windows were elevated to reduce the likelihood of vandalism. In other words, people who didn't like Catholics couldn't successfully throw rocks in an attempt to shatter the windows unless they were really, really strong. But back to the tour.

It was serendipitous (understatement). Unbeknownst to us, the Basilica was usually closed to visitors, but we explored its exterior while a rehearsal for a wedding was taking place. A door to the actual church was open. We entered.

When we walked in, obviously not part of either wedding party, a bored supervisor named Walter gabbed with us. While he was giving us an informal tour of the church, he randomly asked, "Wanna see the crypt?" None of us had ever been asked that question, but okay.

Walter led us to the basement that interred the remains of many former higher-ups of the Philadelphia Catholic Church. He moderately explained the point of the crypt and the significance of those who were deemed eligible to be interred there.

None of us could understand why the tour was so enjoyable; after all, it was a glorified cemetery. Perhaps it was the spontaneity and enthusiasm of our tour guide. Perhaps it was that we experienced it only because we happened to be in the right place at the right time. Speaking for myself, I enjoyed it, but was happy my husband enjoyed it even more.

Lesson learned: The enthusiasm of one person can be infectious, even if his enthusiasm pertains to a bunch of dead guys.

Not Losing My Religion

I have nothing against the unhoused. As a matter of fact, I know several because I serve lunch to many of them every Thursday. However, it was weird to have someone look at me as if I were cowering under a cardboard box desperately trying to stay warm and dry when the sun went down.

On a Sunday morning in Atlanta, I walked to the Immaculate Conception Church. It started to rain like crazy and I arrived looking like a drowned rat. People stared and stared and stared.

I said nothing, but what did I think?

"Everyone, I am here to praise my God. I'm sorry I don't have room in my backpack—or the good sense—to carry an umbrella in rainy Georgia. I grew up in California, where it doesn't rain in summertime.

"Would Jesus stare at me as I worshiped in a puddle of my own making? Doubt it. Would Jesus tell me to go home and clean up before I deigned to appear in His holy house? Doubt it. Doesn't your Bible include James 2:1-4?" (Look it up.)

Lesson learned: For those who thought I didn't belong there due to my waterlogged appearance, my response evokes a line from a reasonably successful movie. "Well, that's just like, your opinion, man."

Yes, We Can Worship and Not Judge

I still regret not attending Mass in Naples, but I was never there on a Sunday. Yes, I know Catholics do daily Mass, but I was young and dumb. Don't tell the Pope.

I did make it to Mass in Bumtruck, Pennsylvania. Earlier in this chapter, I shared my New Orleans and Atlanta Mass experiences that were less than welcoming to outsiders/tourists/whatever-you-wanted-to-call-interlopers-with-disdain. But Bumtruck Catholic Church was very demure. I appreciated the low-key kindness of the small town residents.

If the internet is correct, the church was named The Most Holy Trinity. The congregation treated me as though I was there to worship, not as though I were from only-God-knows-where-probably-sinful-California.

The Mass was a Mass. However, I heard one of my all-time favorite Catholic hymns for the very first time: "One Bread, One Body." Whenever I hear or sing this song, I remember discovering it in a very sweet and humble church.

Of course, memorable songs don't always occur in church. In Memphis in 2019, I and my husband visited Sun Studios. (Elvis Presley sang there and Tom Petty sat on that chair over there, OMG). While we were waiting for the bus to our hotel, I did a quick potty stop at a restaurant located on the bus route. After I did my business, I was thrilled to hear "New Slang," a very sweet song by the Shins. This song is rather obscure, but I remember Memphis every time I hear it.

Lesson learned: Pay attention to the songs I randomly heard; they may occupy a place in my mind forever.

All Day and All of the Night

I walked around Westminster Abbey like a little kid with my eyes bugged out. It is gorgeous in its own right, plus there are a bunch of famous guys interred there. Charles Darwin. Stephen Hawking. Isaac Newton. Charles Dickens. Eighteen British monarchs I was too lazy and uninterested to research. Because I didn't pay attention in my high school British history class, I hadn't heard of most, but sensed that I needed to be impressed.

To further my cultural immersion goal, I decided to attend a Sunday Anglican service. Although I had never attended a service other than a Catholic Mass, I figured it would be kinda-sorta comparable. Um, no.

Catholic Masses run about an hour, and as long as I arrived before the Gospel, "it counts" as fulfilling my Sunday worship obligation. But the Anglicans take two hours to worship the God of their understanding. As hyperactive as I was and am, I had to sit for two hours, with no gymnastics to keep my joints nimble and my butt from hurting. It was stressful. Go Anglicans, but it was hard.

Great songs, I suppose. But unfortunately, I brought my Catholic prejudice into the Abbey and couldn't appreciate their musical worship. Bad me!

Lesson learned: Investigate before attending a service of another faith. If I knew it would be that long, I would have downed a Red Bull before going. Except Red Bull didn't exist in 1985.

Everybody Sit Down

Because I was in Spain and because of my *poquito Espanol*, I understood enough of the local language to be dangerous.

I know some priests are, um, better "homilists" who help us to reflect on the day's readings. Because of that, some Mass attendees have been known to doze off. Witnessed it every once in a while, but I've never done it myself. Really, I promise.

I attended Mass in Barcelona. It was not a particularly notable or famous church. As always, I was pleased to be there. I was also pleased to hear the priest state that "*La materia no importa,*" which translates to "the material possessions do not matter." No argument there, especially because I had nearly no *materia* aside from the contents of my backpack along with my crappy yard sale furniture in storage back in California.

During the homily, a few people actually arose from their seats, some of whom with small children, and walked around the church, purportedly admiring the statues. I guess.

I have attempted to raise three kids in the faith; some of them coped better than others. For that reason, I can understand why some parents wanted to just get through the hour, go back home, and hope Jesus smiled on them for their efforts to raise their children in the faith.

But grown men and women? Did they really want to convey to the priest that he was so boring, they were reduced to sightseeing in a mediocre church? It was just weird. It was probably a regional or cultural thing, but couldn't they just doze off?

Lesson learned: Comparing and contrasting can sometimes be puzzling. And come on, grownups without children must remain seated. Doze if you must.

A Well-Respected Man

After I was off the beaten path of tourist Venice, the city is incredibly peaceful. Very, very easy to get lost in; some supposed "streets" are actually sidewalks.

The canals are quite a sight, although I wouldn't want to be there during rainy season when the city regularly floods. I had never been in a city in which "roads" were not roads, but were instead waterways. Wow.

I am embarrassed to admit I cannot recall the specific church at which I attended Sunday Mass (I should have written it down, sigh), but it was small, cute, and welcoming. As usual, I could follow along sufficiently, perform the gymnastics sufficiently, and pray the Lord's Prayer with my brothers and sisters. Of course, I prayed the latter in English rather than Italian, but I'm sure nobody was surprised. It wasn't hard to figure out I wasn't a local.

Aside from the spiritual nourishment I received, I was amused to notice that the celebrant (Father What-a-Waste...very handsome, but of course celibate) was wearing flip-flops. I had never witnessed a priest wearing such casual footwear, but the August heat in Venice is not for the faint of heart.

Heck, I wore flip-flops too. The rest of my outfit complied with the dress code required to enter Catholic churches throughout Italy (no shorts, shoulders and knees covered). I assume I was wearing a thrift shop T-shirt and a wrinkled thrift shop skirt, but the church granted me admittance even though Mom and Dad would have been horrified.

I could accept Father What-a-Waste's flip-flops. However, because of the floor-length vestments (ceremonial clothing) priests wear, I could only wonder if he was wearing pants. Yes, I know I am supposed to be praying, but come on! I had to occupy myself during a homily given in a language I do not speak.

Lesson learned: It was okay to occasionally let my mind wander when attending Mass in foreign countries. Did the higher-ups know how he was dressed? Did any other parishioners wonder the same thing? Even if they understood Italian?

Hey St. Peter, It Really Feels Like Hell

St. Peter's Basilica, located in Vatican City, is a church. It's a tourist attraction. It's both.

I thought it was a requirement that when in Rome, good Catholics had to attend Mass at St Peter's. Who am I to argue?

Mixed reaction. I did greatly appreciate going to Confession (only had to confess the garden variety sins, nothing awful) and receiving Communion.

But taking photos during Mass? Does anybody have any respect for anything? And this was before the days when people took photos of what they had for breakfast, of who cut them off in the Starbucks line, and of every booger that came out of their respective noses. No idea whether Mass at St. Peter's is a nonstop streaming event these days. I can only hope that, in addition to the no-shorts and no-bare-arms rules, there is a turn-off-your-smartphone rule in effect.

Pope John Paul II was not in Rome that day, but he spoke from his summer residence to the congregation gathered outside of the Basilica proper. He mostly spoke in Italian, but did give a brief address in English.

It was probably good, but of course I had to stand next to Giuseppe, the one atheist in the congregation. It wasn't enough for him to denigrate religion; he also had to make fun of my name. Regarding the latter, apparently he thought we were still in fourth grade. At least he didn't call me Toni Baloney (my elementary school nickname, for crissakes), but he might as well have.

Lesson learned by (apparently) nobody but me: This is Mass, not Disneyland.

Make Me a Channel of Your Peace

It's impossible to ignore the energy of St. Francis while in Assisi, Italy.

No need to feel embarrassed if you don't know who he was. My experience is that many Catholics don't even know how much he rocked. Bad Catholics!

Although most of my vignettes are deadpan and hopefully a bit humorous, visiting Assisi was crazy and I will never forget it. I can provide a brief history about the guy; no need to do intercessory prayers (ask your Catholic friends) unless you choose to do so.

St. Francis was a wealthy man who decided he needed to get rid of all his earthly possessions to follow his Lord. He made this decision after he encountered the San Damiano cross that actually talked to him. Laugh if you must.

He is the patron saint—briefly, a special advocate before God—of animals and the environment. It may sound odd, but St Francis preached to animals even though they couldn't park themselves in an uncomfortable pew and perform the required gymnastics. His feast day is October 4, on which day animals can be brought to church to be blessed. I no longer have pets, but this is another reason he rocked. Philip, Athena, Izzy, Rover (if you're an old dog): have your dog parents bring you to be blessed.

St. Francis's influence infiltrated everything I experienced in Assisi. I spent time in Rome, which is Catholic Central, but I honestly felt like he was giving me a guided tour of his hometown. It was strange and beautiful. Sorry, but Rome doesn't do that. And he must have done something right. He has an order of priests named after him, most of whom similarly rock.

For many years, I thought saints were simply better people than I. Turns out they were imperfect people who performed holy deeds in a humble manner.

The Prayer of St. Francis is sweet, regardless of your faith practices or lack of same. You can throw out the Lord and Divine Master references if necessary, and instead use his words to serve as a resolution to treat your brothers, sisters, neighbors, coworkers, and yourself better. Or less of a jerk...don't let the perfect be the enemy of the good.

Lesson learned: Assisi, holy moley! I could only imagine what a visit to Lourdes or Fatima (other Catholic pilgrimage sites) must be like.

I Also Wept

Fast forward to 2013. We were in Paris and were honestly running out of energy. Our plan for the day was "whatever, as long as it's not as crowded as the Louvre." I think this counts as a church, even though I didn't actually attend a Mass.

We walked across a Seine River bridge and bought a combination ticket for the Conciergerie, a French prison which once housed Marie Antoinette, and the Sainte-Chapelle, which appeared to be a generic, beige-looking chapel from the outside.

The Conciergerie was so boring that I will put you to sleep if I describe it. Let's just move on to Sainte-Chapelle. Okay, whatever. But when we ascended the staircase to the main chapel, I gasped. Literally. Not figuratively.

The Sainte-Chapelle was originally intended to house Christian relics — most notably, Jesus's crown of thorns — but instead it evolved into the most stunning stained-glass display I have ever, ever, ever seen.

Believe it or don't, over 1000 smallish panels depict each of the books of the Bible. Aside from my sheer astonishment at the effort expended to create the Bible vignettes, the sun's rays created an incredibly brilliant display. I didn't want to leave and it took me more than a few minutes to do so. Thankfully, my family declined to drag me out kicking and screaming.

For those unfamiliar with the Bible, the shortest sentence that describes the life of Jesus consists of two words: "Jesus wept." He would surely weep with joy at the beauty of this chapel. If you ask the internet about only one of my memories, this is the one. I even bought the commemorative coffee table book; the postcard remains on my refrigerator to this day. You don't even need to believe in God to marvel at its beauty.

Lesson apparently not learned: I have two friends who visited Paris since we were there. Despite my begging and pleading, neither of them included this magical place on their itineraries. No idea what I did wrong.

Intermittently Glorious Food and Drink

I feel sorry for picky eaters.

As you have figured out by now, I was on a budget and couldn't even entertain the idea of eating at a Michelin-starred restaurant. I and my husband have since eaten at a couple of them; IMO, they are generally overrated. Learn to cook. It's not that hard.

I had resolved to not subsist on fast food. God bless Wendy's salad bar (see below), but I was determined to eat actual local specialties whenever possible, even if the locals stared at me. Hey, I could stare back. "Why don't you live in California? It's much better! There's a reason it costs a fortune to live there!"

Back to the picky eaters rant. Readers, there is so much great food in the world. I get that we like what we like, but you should try chickpeas and asparagus for Sunday brunch. It's great. And easy. Yes, I know it sounds weird.

Culinary adventures. Let's do it.

Wendy's Was the Fast Food Rocker

It's entirely possible I would have starved if not for Wendy's all-you-can-eat salad bar. When I arrived in town hungry (which was most of the time), my first goal is to locate Wendy's. No smartphones back then; I would have to pay attention or even ask a local. Yikes, how old am I?

I don't go to Wendy's anymore, but they had an opulent spread of salad greens, ham, cheese, and other accoutrements. When I patronized them, I would literally spend two hours stuffing myself. And no, they are not paying me to say this, probably because they don't even have a salad bar anymore. And they would probably be angry because I ate all I could…and more.

At least I didn't hide any food in my backpack to save for later. I had my dignity.

Lesson learned: All-You-Can-Eat is your friend…unless it's fried fish. Read on about Gainesville.

When Life Gives You Lemons, Eat Crawfish

I serendipitously arrived in Chicago in time for the Taste of Chicago, a huge festival that continues to this day. The free concert lineup included Glenn Frey of the Eagles (I know, you hate the Eagles). The lineup also included Chuck Berry. Although he was great, I feared he'd break a hip while doing his signature dance that seemed inadvisable for a man his age. I was genuinely relieved that his duck walk resulted in no broken bones. How did Chuck do it when he was only slightly younger than I am now? Go Chuck!

I was thrilled to stumble upon a food booth that was serving boiled crawfish. If you are unfamiliar with them, they look like giant bugs, which is why they are sometimes referred to as mudbugs. To eat them, I had to "pinch the tail and suck the head." Really.

Crawfish are a kinda-sorta open secret. They are commonly consumed in Louisiana along with a handful of other locales, but not so much elsewhere. When I got mine, people looked at me and even inquired, "What the heck is that?" I tried to explain how yummy they are, but they seemed unconvinced. Poor them.

Great food, great music. One of my better days.

Lessons learned:

- If others didn't want the crawfish, there was more left for me.

- Yes, Glenn Frey, I officially belong to the city. Such a pleasant surprise to see you perform your beautiful song without having to purchase an overpriced ticket. Sigh and RIP.

The Wonton Song

One of Led Zeppelin's songs was titled "The Wanton Song." Profound, I guess? But I and my high school friends invariably pronounced it as the "The Wonton Song"--you know, the Chinese dumpling. Thankfully, none of us had a driver's license yet. For that reason, we couldn't run you over; the wise authorities had declined to let us behind the wheels of our parents' respective cars.

Thai restaurants do wontons differently than Chinese restaurants, but they still do them. For that reason and the mispronounced Led Zep song, here we go.

On an adventurous culinary streak. Because I ate at the Wendy's salad bar for a couple of days, I had a couple of extra bucks. Let's do an Authentic Thai Restaurant located in an Authentic Chicago Neighborhood.

I'd never eaten at a Thai restaurant, so I crossed my fingers and ordered from the menu, having absolutely no idea what I ordered. Because I was the only person using an actual fork, I knew it was an authentic place. I am still unable to use chopsticks, but I guess it's just my lack of manual dexterity. My entree arrived and I was ready to explore the possible flavor enhancements.

Tiny peppers? Wow, I've never had those. And they're called bird's-eye chilies? Such a benign name. If they are popular enough that the restaurant routinely provides them, they will probably spice up my entree to a pleasant extent.

HOLY CRAP! HOLY CRAP! HOLY CRAP! I took one bite of those tiny peppers and thought I was going to die. I subsequently learned that the smaller the pepper, the more potent it is. But that didn't help me during this particular dinner. I hope nobody saw my panicked state. I don't think I spit it out in horror, but I may have. You know, the not-wanting-to-die thing.

At the time, I didn't know about the Scoville scale, which rates the heat level of chili peppers. I subsequently found out that the bird's-eye chili heat level is 50,000-100,000 units. Compare that to a jalapeño, which checks in at 2,500-8,000 units. Okay, there are a few chilis which check in at much higher levels (I will never-ever-ever try the Carolina Reaper and Trinidad Scorpion), but I was surprised that flames were not spewing from my mouth as I continued my futile attempt to eat my food.

My husband has told me that many Thai restaurants provide a warning label regarding these peppers. However, because I was the only White girl eating with a fork, my guess is that the other patrons knew how potent these peppers are. The Thai owners were content to simply laugh at the clueless tourists when all hell broke loose in their respective mouths.

Lesson learned: Toni! Adventurous eating is good, but please try just one bite first.

OMG, Chili Spaghetti

Of course, I primarily came to Cincinnati to see a baseball game. I was able to find a zero-star motel across the Ohio River in Covington, Kentucky. I have been told that Covington is quite the affluent area now, but back then, no. At least, not in the area I scoured for a place to sleep.

I had to barricade the door because its lock was malfunctioning. On the upside, it did have an actual bed, bathtub, and TV. Of course, because the desk clerk was behind bulletproof glass, I quickly figured out the necessity of the barricade.

In hindsight, it's puzzling that this California girl assumed that large Midwest cities were polluted and smokestack-laden, because Cincinnati is very pretty. Along the river, there was the Serpentine Wall, a gorgeous paved riverwalk that offered places to sit and relax. Not gorgeous in freezing December, I suppose, but in July, yeah.

My pre-travel research didn't educate me, but chili is a thing in Cincinnati. I went to one of the city's chili parlors and ordered a "five-way chili"--spaghetti, chili, beans, onions, cheese--and took it to the Serpentine Wall to enjoy an alfresco lunch on a sunny day.

(If that sounds like waaay too much food, you can instead order a two-, three-, or four-way chili. Some Cincinnati residents even refer to these ordering options as "the ways." Very cute, IMO.)

It's such a kick to experience regional food. I really wondered why Cincinnati kept its chili a secret. Why does Rochester keep its garbage plate a secret? Why does Philadelphia keep its cheesesteak a secret? Oh wait, Philly doesn't. The evolving question is that why do some areas keep their culinary specialties a secret and others do not?

If you're ever in Cincinnati, go to a chili parlor, even if they use cinnamon in their recipe. Yes, I know that sounds weird, and it is. When I prepare it at home, I leave it out.

Lesson learned: I needed to continue seeking out regional specialties. Life is too short for Burger King.

Make That Connection

I was eating at a fairly nice New Orleans restaurant that had actual cloth napkins.

Although I barely remember what I had for dinner last night, I absolutely remember eating soft-shell crabs 37 years ago. OMG, who thought of these? I have always loved trying new meals, especially if they are as seriously good as soft-shell crabs. Ramen for the next three days? Who cares?

As I was eating on my own, a very personable patron invited me to join him and other tourists at their table. Wait, what? But I decided to join them and we had a wonderful time.

Greg became a very close friend of mine. Randomly, we discovered we had the same birthday, although in different years. I visited him at his home in Boston; he subsequently moved to California. We lived a manageable distance from one another and were able to hang out quite a bit. Because he was a nice and decent person, of course he couldn't be a boyfriend. But I attended his wedding and he attended mine.

Lesson learned: Dining alone? I could ask someone to join me! I will always admire Greg for his boldness, and it honestly never occurred to me to approach strangers who could become my friends. Unfortunately, we have lost touch. Miss you, Greg. Hope your life is going well. I hate losing touch with friends I thought would be there forever.

Frozen Heart

It was a not-so-great way to call attention to myself.

I walked into a Louisville bar at happy hour, discovered that I was the only White girl in there, and ordered 2-for-1 frozen margaritas. I doubt the bartender had made a margarita any time in the previous year because they seriously looked like Slurpees (ask your elders or go to a 7-11).

I sheepishly drank or spooned my drinks, convinced that everyone was looking at the WTF White girl, which was probably not true.

Why did I think other people cared about me that much? They were most likely engrossed in conversations with their companions or worrying about their own dilemmas. Not worrying about me. On the other hand, they could have been laughing at me because I was obviously a tourist and out of place.

Regardless, I am quite confident that none of the patrons ordered their next drink by indicating "I'll have what she's having." That would be a great movie line, am I right? Wink, wink.

Lessons learned:

- The most awkward experiences were the ones I retained.

- For crissakes, Toni, read the room before you order a drink.

Betcha Can't Really Eat That Much

After my Tom Petty semi-immersion experience (refer to "Yeah, This Is Better Than Working"), it was dinnertime. I was intrigued by a restaurant named Captain Louie's Galley. Because the name did not include the word "Gator," I was puzzled why it was allowed to do business in Gainesville. That said, I was especially intrigued by the four favorite words in a frugal traveler's culinary universe: "all you can eat." I am so there!

As I mentioned earlier in this chapter, Wendy's salad bar was consistently my friend. I'm sure the management asked themselves what they were thinking when they offered such bounty for a ridiculously low price and I spent at least two hours availing myself of it. The joke was on them. Take that!

But moving on to Captain Louie's, the joke was on me.

I resolved to eat all the fried fish I could. The fish was very yummy, but how much fried fish can a 22-year-old with a normal-sized stomach actually eat? Perhaps a linebacker twice my size could consume enough to cause management to question their generous offer, but me? I think I ate two pieces, maybe three. As I limped out in a food coma, I could only imagine management's reaction. "Bahaha, we sure made money on this naive tourist."

Lesson learned: All-you-can-eat menus are not offered out of the goodness of the management's heart. Unless hungry linebackers streamed into Captain Louie's, the restaurant was going to make a profit.

I Thought Everybody Would Know My Name

Those of us of a certain age know that "Cheers" was an extremely popular TV show that aired from 1982 through 1993 on Thursdays at 9 PM. Although it had an unremarkable start, it ultimately became known as "appointment TV," a show for which everyone could clear their schedule in order to watch. VCRs were still moderately unaffordable, so in that era, viewers had to watch a show when it was broadcast. How sick is that?

While in Boston, I needed to go to the Cheers Bar's theoretical location, just to say I did. Remarkably, its exterior looked virtually identical to the location featured on the show, and it was indeed in the basement of the main building. Its name was not Cheers; it was the Bull and Finch Pub.

I descended the stairs not knowing what to expect; after all, TV tends to exaggerate. But whaddaya know, it too looked almost identical to the TV show set, although it was quite a bit smaller. And no Ted Danson, Shelley Long, Woody Harrelson, or other "Cheers" cast members, not that I was expecting to see them. I mean, duh.

Sat down, dutifully ordered an affordable drink, waited for the warm and welcoming atmosphere to surface, and it did. For the first and (so far) last time in my life, I gabbed with an actual private investigator. Although our conversation was completely G-rated, he gave me his phone number and of course I never called him. Geez, he was old enough to be my dad. But a very pleasant dad.

Apparently the Bull and Finch became quite the tourist attraction as the TV show's popularity increased, but thankfully I was able to experience it when it was still just a local bar and didn't sell souvenirs. No idea how the production team managed to convey the vibe of the real-life venue, but they sure did.

Lessons learned:

- Sometimes art does imitate life. When I left the Bull and Finch, not everybody knew my name (listen to the "Cheers" theme song). But one person did.

- Tourist destinations can actually be fun, even if Sam Malone isn't the bartender (ask your elders).

Unexpected Protein

After I proverbially woke up from the train wreck that was Madrid's Museo del Prado (refer to "Hanging in the Gallery"), my priority was—what else?—food. Let's go to a tapas bar, which was not necessarily a bar that served alcohol, just a place to get cute portions of various Spanish appetizers.

It was only around 6:00 PM. Because the Spanish didn't even think of dinner before 10:00 PM, I should have known that meant yesterday's moderately edible leftovers. Apparently, I didn't. But I assume that's what I got.

My meatballs were good enough…that is, until I encountered an unexpected source of protein: a fly or two or three. Really.

How do I handle this? Of course, you know by now that because I was on a serious budget, I couldn't spend a lot of money on restaurants. Of course, you know by now that I didn't want to be a fussy American. But flies? With wings and everything? Decisions, decisions.

Perhaps the locals knew better than to eat at this particular tapas bar, which was arguably a health department violation, although I was unsure if the city actually had a health department at the time. Perhaps the locals knew that if patrons got what they deserved if they ate dinner before 10:00 PM.

But gosh, I was not a resident; I was just a bored and hungry American trying to eat some semblance of authentic local cuisine. Please spare me from another Big Mac with the cryptic special sauce! However, I had to debate whether I really wanted to say *"Camarero, hay moscas en mis albondigas."* ("Waiter, there are flies in my meatballs.") In the end, I decided to push the yucky ones to one side and eat the remainder. I officially wouldn't starve.

Lesson learned: Sometimes I just needed to shut up. And avert my eyes.

Pigs' Ears? Whaaat?

Are we seeing a pattern here regarding cheap Madrid food?

In my eternal pursuit of weird food, I was drawn to *orejas del cerdo* (pigs' ears).

After my *albondiga* adventure that involved fly corpses, I still hadn't given up. Pigs' ears? Who thought of eating those? This was even before the nose-to-tail movement, in which creative chefs such as Fergus Henderson made virtually every animal body part suitable for consumption. He even wrote a couple of cookbooks about his efforts, and Anthony Bourdain was sufficiently impressed that he gave him a shoutout. (RIP, Anthony.)

Using my *poquito Espanol*, I confidently ordered them. And they tasted like bacon. Who knew? It wasn't even a weird experience, just a bacon experience.

How can I eat weird food if it really isn't that weird? I theoretically could have eaten *orejas del cerdo* in Florence; they might have just called it "bacon."

Lesson learned: Avoiding fast food joints didn't necessarily mean I was eating exotic food. And it's entirely possible that anything gleaned from a pig will taste like bacon.

The Wurst Is Yet to Come

If I have to sum up my food experience in Germany, I ate my first Big Mac at a Munich McDonald's.

My family almost never ate fast food. During our summer vacation, we would get a bucket of Kentucky Fried Chicken, now KFC and not as good as it was Back in the Day. We would also get Round Table Pizza once or twice a year. I imagine it was because Dad would picture his old-country Sicilian mother rolling over in her grave at the thought of his feeding her grandchildren such garbage. "Come on, Angelo! Pasta, pasta, pasta! What is wrong with you?"

Although Munich's Bavarian pastries were great, the wurst (which I had begun to pronounce "worst") looked awful and disgusting. Weird sausages that were varying shades of drab colors. Had any Germans been to Italy and eaten their amazing food? Sorry, Munich.

I ended up going to McDonald's. Bad tourist; I should partake of the local grub! I really hated the idea of choosing American fast food instead of trying local (alleged) specialties. I was so judgmental of Americans eating bacon and eggs in Florence.

But ewww, the wurst. I just couldn't.

Weird to order at McDonald's and see beer on the menu, but then, some Germans have beer at breakfast. Again, ewww.

Lesson learned: Try the food, but know my limits. I really hated the idea of American chains in other countries, but McDonald's ensured I wouldn't starve, and for that I am thankful. That said, I don't think I've eaten a Big Mac since.

Forty Cups of Coffee

Yep, the Leaning Tower is a thing. Thankfully, I was able to visit once again with my family in 2013. It's a bit of an effort to ascend the staircase, but worth it. Its stairs have been worn down by the sheer number of visitors who have made the journey. And these are solid stone steps, not cheap plywood.

Saw the Tower, but now what? Oh yeah, I needed to figure out where I would eat and sleep.

I wandered around looking for a room. Okay, this one seems promising. I entered and pretended I could speak Italian (actually, I absorbed a bit due to my study of Spanish and French, albeit to a lesser extent). My grammatical and descriptive request in Italian: "*Pension?*" My grammatical and exhausted request in my mind's silent English: "Can I just pay for the room and be done with it? I am hot and tired."

The young employee took me up to a godawful room in an attic. Not only would I seriously have to crouch down to walk across the room, I would have to manually bail water into the toilet in order to flush it. I declined the room, and the employee referred to me as *"cattiva Americana"* (bad female American). I would not be bullied into accepting a room only slightly more comfortable than a prison cell. Thankfully, he apologized and referred to me as *"buona Americana"* (good female American). Apparently, chivalry wasn't entirely dead.

I continued wandering and found a better and more comfortable place. After checking in, I tried to figure out what to do. No TV, no baseball, no internet in the dark ages.

Espresso! Yeah, that should be fun!

At the time, espresso was just catching on in our nation, but had long been a part of Italians' daily rituals. I decided to visit several espresso bars, not realizing some menu items included alcohol shots for those customers who wished to kick up their beverages. When I ordered a *caffe corretto* in an effort to be adventurous, the guy asked which shot I wanted. Wait, what? Is that what *corretto* means? I changed my order.

Guess what happened after I visited several espresso bars. I was so caffeinated that I could not sleep. I imagined this must be what cocaine is like.

In my state of insomnia, I realized the staff locked us guests in for the night and went home. OMG, no adult supervision? What if the place caught on fire? Is this where I would meet my demise? Aside from the espresso buzz, I now had the fear of imminent death to keep me awake. In hindsight, it reminds me of a Flintstones episode in which Fred and Barney had to spend the night in a possibly haunted mansion in order to inherit a serious amount of money from a creepy uncle. Only, in my case, there was no inheritance and no uncle involved...just not dying. At any rate, it was a long night. And I slept for two hours at the most.

Lesson learned: Not a good idea to drink forty espressos--okay, I'm exaggerating--unless an all-night midterm cramming session is necessary.

Breakfast in America? But We Aren't in America!

Loved Florence, but some restaurants served bacon and egg breakfasts when Italians content themselves with brioche and espresso. Pander much to tourists? In all fairness, perhaps Americans missed their usual breakfast fare. But why come to Italy if you still crave your American breakfast? Why not just stay home? Sigh.

After eating the regionally appropriate brioche and espresso for breakfast, my biggest laugh was on an early morning stroll into a tiny local grocery store. My comment to the proprietor in my *poco Italiano*: *"Molti Americani, si?"* ("Plenty of Americans, am I right?") I caught him totally off-guard and both of us had a huge laugh.

Lesson learned: For crissakes, don't eat bacon and eggs in Italy. Plenty of those breakfasts in America. Eat the brioche and drink the espresso, or hang your head in shame at the cultural insensitivity. You be you.

I Don't Need No Stinking Menu

"Let's Go Europe," the late and lamented budget travel guide, said *Ostario da Toto* would be a "truly Sicilian dining experience." One word: understatement. I already briefly described a fun Palermo restaurant experience (refer to "Somewhere Under Heaven"), but this is even better.

A restaurant with no menu. Really? I couldn't understand the waiter, and a nice old guy tried to help. After that exercise in futility, the waiter had me follow him into the kitchen and point to what I wanted. I was so blindsided by the culture shock, I pointed to some random pasta.

When I was served my lunch, the nice old guy shared his lemon soda with me. As I stuffed myself, the staff and patrons expressed their concerns about how I was not eating enough. (Okay, it was all in Italian, but I could get their drift, possibly from their animated gestures.) In Italy, the pasta is a first course, but my tummy remained the same size it's always been. Pasta was good enough; no second or third course was necessary.

I paid the waiter; he smiled very sincerely and even shook my hand. It could have been a heartwarming movie ending; it was so very Sicilian.

Lesson learned: Many people in less-touristed destinations embrace Americans and treat them kindly. (I know Palermo is a cruise ship port now, but it wasn't Back in the Day.) And walking into a restaurant kitchen to pick out what I wanted? How many people have done that?

Take Me Out to the Ballgame

If you're not a baseball fan, I know what you're saying to yourself. "Self, why should I bother reading this chapter? I don't care if name-of-pitcher threw a no-hitter…whatever that is. I don't care if name-of-batter had a historic clutch hit or home run…whatever those are. Seeing-eye single? What the heck is that?"

You should bother because ballparks are a microcosm of our culture. You should bother because you can vicariously witness your neighbors at their best…or worst.

Overpriced beer, overpriced hot dogs, overpriced merchandise, plus crowds that are as varied as their host cities. Some are extremely knowledgeable, others simply worship at the altar of their team and spend too much on overpriced stuff. Yes, a lot of baseball games are boring, but the good ones? Just as my college psychology professor taught me, "intermittent gratification is the most addictive of all."

I had resolved to visit as many ballparks as I could. In the 1980s, most were concrete behemoths. If you want to see a present-day example, visit the Oakland Coliseum. I still enjoy going there, but sigh. Even Sal Bando, the Oakland A's late-great team captain during The Great Years of the early 1970s (see below), described it as a "mausoleum." BTW, even though the team is allegedly moving to Las Vegas, they will always be the Oakland A's to me.

My goal was to compare and contrast my experience in various locales, as well as to enhance my bragging rights. I think and hope I have succeeded. Plenty of ballpark experiences, but I have to start with the prequel.

Dad was notoriously, um, "frugal." We periodically had family trips to see the Swingin' A's at the Oakland Coliseum. The team won three straight World Series in the 1970s, but I was too young and dumb to appreciate the history I was witnessing.

Dad was far too frugal to buy actual good seats for his family of six. He was also too frugal to buy stadium-priced hot dogs for us. Solution? Homemade eggplant sandwiches, hopefully in a cooler but not sure. No, I am not making this up.

I may have gone hungry, and I likely envied other patrons who were eating the stadium's hot dogs; at least they were (probably) hot. None of us kids liked eggplant sandwiches, for crissakes. But I didn't dare whine; that wasn't how we interacted with our parents. Kids today.

I hope I can convey the weird and wonderful experiences I have had at ballparks. Who cares if you're not a fan? Maybe I can convert you. The pitch clock, which was recently instituted, has made the game faster...trust me.

Play ball!

Cheering for the Pirates, Not Talking Like One

As I previously stated, my misguided understanding was that Pittsburgh was a polluted, putrid pit. That changed; I was pleasantly shocked at how pretty the city was. I walked over to Three Rivers Stadium stadium a few hours before game time to explore.

Who knew I would be able to walk into the center field gate and wander around? Who knew I could stand in center field, pretend I was Marvell Wynne, and pretend the empty stands were full of fans hoping I would catch the opposing team's winning home run and salvage the victory?

Choose your cultural reference if baseball is not your thing. Walk-on role at Central Perk in "Friends?" Defeating Littlefinger Baelish in "Game of Thrones?" Cellmate of Piper Chapman in "Orange is the New Black?" It was that exciting. And nobody stopped me.

The game was fun. In particular, I loved the pregame announcement. "The Pirates respect your right to express your opinion, but please refrain from using obscenities."

The Pirates' organ player cracked him- or herself up in several ways. When a player actually named Jim Morrison came to bat, he would play "Touch Me." When Bob Walk came to bat, he would play "Walk of Life." Okay, maybe you had to be there, or be familiar with the Doors and Dire Straits. But I got it and also cracked up.

By the end of the night, the Pirates had humiliated the Dodgers with a score of 16-2. Because I was a Dodger fan at the time, I enjoyed engaging in a lot of shouting matches with a bunch of adorable little boys. I did remind them that the Pirates were still in last place. They would ultimately finish the season in the same unfortunate position.

Lesson learned: Sometimes I didn't need permission to have a memorable experience. And sometimes, the staff simply doesn't care.

Lesson not learned: I am certain I encountered an actual baseball player in downtown Pittsburgh on game day. Why the heck didn't I approach him? He was just a mere mortal, albeit an extremely well-paid mortal. In recent years, I encountered Ray Fosse (a legendary Oakland A's baseball announcer) and didn't approach him either. What was wrong with me?

Cubs, Woo!

Somehow I managed to attend eight games at Chicago's Wrigley Field. It lived up to its characterization that it wasn't a "stadium," but a "ballpark." Pretty sure this sentiment was attributed to Harry Caray, the Cubs' longtime announcer and seventh-inning-stretch singer. They now have a statue of him near the center field bleachers, but I'm proud that I experienced the real guy, even if at a distance. No, I never met him.

I was rather, um, apprehensive when I first arrived in The Windy City. So big. So busy. So intimidating.

My immediate goal was to get to the ballpark. When I boarded the subway, nicknamed the "El," I asked someone for help with the correct route. He grumpily replied, "Follow me," and I got there unscathed. Ultimately, Chicago is a big small town, and people are generally sweet. Thank you, what's-your-name; I will always remember your kindness.

Wrigley Field had a vibe like no other. The fans could be classified in two groups: the rabid ones who could recall every bit of

Take Me Out to the Ballgame

Cubs minutiae known to mankind, and the bleacher bums, there for the beer they could drink unapologetically at 11 AM (favorite beer vendor shout: "Who's ready for breakfast?") Some have characterized the bleachers as the best singles bar in Chicago, but I was just there for a cheap seat. Five bucks. Really.

The fans generally assumed their team would stink—the marketing department even promoted the "lovable losers" narrative—and they usually did, although they had their moments. At the very least, they weren't as awful as the Pirates were during the 1985 season. And then there's Ronnie "Woo Woo" Wickers. Yes, he is sometimes irritating, but so passionate. Basically an unhoused guy at one point, Cubs fans financially support him because of his love for the team.

Their fans started a dubious tradition. If the opposing team hit a home run and a fan caught it, the fan must immediately throw it back. Who cares if it was hit by a future Hall of Famer, or even Barry Bonds, and might be worth a ton of money? Doesn't matter; if it was scored against the home team, it needed to be rejected. This tradition started in 1969 because a fan was offended when he unsuccessfully tried to return a home run ball Hank Aaron had hit the previous year. (For the uninitiated, Aaron is the actual all-time home run hitter; he didn't need no stinking steroids.)

Fast forward to 2006. My husband and I went to a Cubs game because we were in town for a Tom Petty concert later that night. I'm sure the Tom Petty aspect isn't a shock.

Aside from the ticket prices skyrocketing (five bucks, bahaha), Wrigley never changes. It was still pretty, and Ronnie Wickers was still in the bleachers repeatedly chanting "Cubs, woo!" The team

141

even gave him an honorary uniform and he is still attending games in his eighties. Go Ronnie!

Because Harry Caray is no longer with us, guest singers participate in the seventh-inning stretch rendition of "Take Me Out to the Ballgame." In 2006, the guest singer was, of all people, Tommy Lasorda of the Los Angeles Dodgers—in other words, the manager of the Evil Empire. Whaaat?

A very polite man sat in front of us with his dad; their overheard exchanges were heartwarming. However, when Tommy started to sing, he was compelled to yell "F*CK YOU, LASORDA!" And then he apologized to me for his profanity. After all, he was a very polite man.

Lesson learned: Although bleacher seats are waaay more than five bucks these days, it is quite an experience to witness how some fans love their team. I can only imagine how the Cubs faithful lost their minds when they finally won the World Series in 2016, "only" 108 years since the last victory.

Beer Drinkers and Hell Raisers

The Chicago White Sox were and are the red-headed stepchildren of Chicago baseball. Okay, the Cubs are obviously the sentimental favorite team among the city's baseball fans, but how many Cubs T-shirts must I witness while doing other unrelated stuff—art museums, lunch, walking tours? Of course, I needed to go to Comiskey Park just to express my fatigue at the collective Cubs love. If I rooted for the opposing team, what could go wrong?

At the time, I had no idea Charles Comiskey (the ballpark's namesake) was such a tightwad. After watching "Eight Men Out," I discovered he ranks among the most egregiously awful owners of a baseball team…and they named the park after him. Sigh.

I should have known Comiskey Park could be rather, um, rough around the edges. In 1979, there was a "Disco Demolition Night" promotion, in which a crate filled with disco records was detonated after the first game of a doubleheader (two games played back-to-back). Chaos ensued. Obviously, no 1970s disco fans in the stands, but I'm sure the ballpark crew didn't anticipate the chaos. Understandably, they never tried that again.

I showed up at the stadium prepared to root for the Boston Red Sox. Weren't we all friends? Apparently not. I hate the taste and smell of beer, but somehow I became drenched and stinky after some White Sox fans decided to show their contempt by pouring their beer on me. I guess I was louder than I realized. But guys, I wasn't a Cubs fan. It should have absolved me.

The joke was on the White Sox fans because the Red Sox won. But I had to return to my zero-star room smelling like beer. Did I already establish that I hate the smell of beer?

Lesson learned: Some ballparks do not welcome opposing fans in the spirit of friendly rivalry. I tried to assume the White Sox fans simply made a mistake, or perhaps had one too many. Geez, with the price of ballpark beer, why would someone want to waste one just to spite me? But did I believe that? No. They weren't Phillies fans, but even Phillies fans never poured beer on me.

There's No Substitute for Reds

Aside from Cincinnati being surprisingly beautiful in general, Riverfront Stadium — now replaced by Great American Ballpark-- was also a surprise.

Yes, it was a concrete behemoth. However, "riverfront" wasn't a figure of speech; it was located on the banks of the Ohio River. Unfortunately, I could only see a microscopic view of the river while at the game, but I felt my stress vanish as I made my way to the stadium across a bridge on a pleasant summer night.

Unfortunately, the stadium builders apparently didn't realize it would be awesome to incorporate a great view of the river into the fans' experience. Fortunately, the San Francisco Giants figured that out when they built Oracle Park fifteen years later. I wanted to be cynical the first time I attended a game there, but even I continue to be captivated by how it showcases the view of the bay located just outside the venue. Night games can get horribly cold, but the Giants' predecessor stadium was worse, even though the tickets were way cheaper.

Back to Riverfront. In the 1970s, the Reds were known as "The Big Red Machine" and are considered one of the greatest teams ever, and Game 6 of the 1975 World Series is reputed to be the best game in Series history. That said, I encountered that team's catcher, Johnny Bench, at the 1984 All-Star Game and he was horribly mean to a very polite young boy. The Big Red Machine's lineup may have been great players, but they weren't necessarily decent people.

In 1985, the Reds weren't quite as good, but were still a contender. The stadium itself was a bit forgettable, but the night was pleasant and it was a good game.

The Cincinnati fans didn't randomly cheer "We're #1!" The team had to play well to earn the fans' accolades. And they did. Go Reds!

Lesson learned by Oracle Park: Don't build the ballpark in a manner that obstructs a glorious view.

Even the Losers

I was only in Milwaukee long enough to see a couple of baseball games. Initially, I was not impressed, just disappointed. I tried to like Milwaukee's stadium crowd. But the people were very, um, within themselves. I would even make offhand remarks and they were ill-received. California girls...do they ever shut up?

However, my cooler head prevailed the next day; I probably was just tired and cynical when I arrived at the ballpark. There were good things; for example, the German band who played pre-game. The cheese. The sausage. The ethnicity of the experience was tremendous.

There was a very impressive aspect of how Milwaukee County Stadium did business. Rather than let profiteering vendors gouge the fans, the Brewers permit community organizations to manage the various food and beverage options. The profits benefit the organizations in their various efforts. This effort continues to this day at their new ballpark: American Family Field. Go Brewers! Is this hard?

1985 was a bad year for the Brewers (thank God for the Cleveland team), but their stadium was comparable to having a picnic in the park with neighbors. I was only a kinda-sorta-but-not-really neighbor, maybe an interloper. Or not. Perhaps I was just sleep-deprived when I wrote my first impression. And it was very sweet to witness a mom and daughter share a day at the ballpark.

And even though 1985 was awful, they beat the Yankees. It's always a good day when the Yankees lose.

Lesson (almost no sports organization) learned: Why can't more professional sports teams permit nonprofits to raise money by operating food concessions? This is a great idea, and I wish it would go viral.

Motor City Madhouse

Am I really using a Ted Nugent song as a vignette title? What have I become? At least I didn't use "Wang Dang Sweet Poontang" or "Wango Tango," both of which are actual song titles.

Bless me, Father, for I have sinned. I was a big Nugent fan in high school; I even got his autograph at a promotional appearance. However, that was before I realized one of his biggest hits was about brutally beating his girlfriend. And before he became waaay too conservative for me.

Okay, I have to admit the "Stranglehold" guitar solo was great. The lyrics, not so much, now that I know better. (Not-so-fun fact: An actual 1970s Nugent quote that appeared in the late, great *Creem* magazine: "I'd rape a nun if she got in my way." But I was still a fan. Teenagers, sigh.)

Detroit was not frightening; well, perhaps, a little bit. I was relieved that the Greyhound station had a secure waiting area located in the women's restroom. Probably not a bad idea to err on the side of caution.

I arrived in town on a Sunday morning. Greektown was very ethnic; imagine that. I was able to attend a Latin Mass for the first time—in Greektown, but okay. It was actually quite moving.

I am too young to remember when all Masses were spoken in Latin. In the 1960s, the Second Vatican Council decided that they should be given in the local language so the parishioners would know what the heck was going on. Previously, the only indication was when bells were rung to signify the most holy moments of the centerpiece prayer.

After I fulfilled my Sunday obligation, it was time to worship at the church of baseball. Off to Tiger Stadium. At the time, Wrigley Field and Fenway Park were supposedly the Greatest Ballparks in the History of Mankind. However, the Tiger Stadium bleachers were much rowdier than I expected. The designated cheerleader was "Detroit's Own Doctor Geek". The bleacher bums' profane shouts were a parody of a "tastes great, less filling" beer commercial popular in the 1980s. Left section shout: "F*CK YOU!" Right section response: "EAT SH*T!"

I thought I simply had to check off Tiger Stadium on my ballpark list, but what an unexpected blast. Why, why, why were Wrigley and Fenway getting all the baseball love? And are three why's enough?

I would love to visit Comerica Park, the Tigers' present-day stadium, but their original stadium is a tough act to follow. At any rate, go Tigers! They haven't won the World Series since 1984, so they're due. I think?

Lesson learned: Don't always believe the pundits. Now that the old Tiger Stadium doesn't exist, I am thankful I was able to experience it, especially when it was such an unexpected surprise. For crissakes, I thought I was just going to a game, not a happily chaotic madhouse. I don't even remember who won, but it didn't matter.

Meet Me in St. Louis, But Not at the Fair

Back in the Day, the San Francisco Bay Area was the home of two—count 'em, two--concrete behemoths inconveniently located in the respective Bumtruck parts of its two baseball cities. Imagine my surprise when I was strolling through downtown St. Louis and all of a sudden a ballpark appeared. It was as beautiful as my car wash boss Pat told me it was. Busch Stadium was before its time. The stadium I visited was demolished in 2005, but the new stadium is just south. Probably same vibe.

Aside from it spontaneously erupting in the middle of downtown, it featured a Cardinals Hall of Fame. This type of ballpark museum is more common now, but not Back Then. It was a kick to learn about characters such as Rogers Hornsby, one of the best batters in baseball history and also a player-manager—he hit a grand slam (a home run with the bases loaded) while he was a manager?! There are no player-managers these days, but I wish there were.

Surprisingly, Cardinals fans were generally nondescript. At least I got into a shouting match with a young guy in which we debated who sucked the most: Dodgers or Cardinals. Spoiler alert: Dodgers won. And no, I didn't taunt him. Ultimately, I have manners.

Lessons learned:

- Some baseball cities are appreciated because of their ballparks. But I also appreciated St. Louis because I could sleep in a very nice hotel…perhaps two stars?
- Go Rogers Hornsby!

What's the Matter With Kansas City?

Actually, not much! I showed up for baseball, but was struck by the sheer number of fountains throughout the city. Heck, even the Royals' Kauffman Stadium had fountains in the outfield. And go KC; its stadium is one of the few not named for a corporation. I love that.

The Royals fans were a rather subdued bunch, politely applauding when their team did well. Not yelling "YOU SUCK" when they didn't. Not taunting the opponent.

But wow, when George Brett, who was the undisputed star of the team at the time, came up to bat, the stadium erupted. And the Royals ultimately prevailed over the Milwaukee Brewers.

Aside from baseball and fountains, I learned (duh) that Kansas City was famous for its barbecue. Unfortunately, my food budget didn't permit me to try it. Oh well, beef-flavored Top Ramen is a good substitute, right? Actually, no. Sigh.

When I was leaving town, I went to a happy hour for a few minutes while awaiting my bus departure. I found myself sitting next to a man who was absolutely, incredibly intoxicated. Three sheets to the wind? Let's make that four. And it was barely 4:00.

Of course, he was more than ready to talk to whomever would listen. That would kinda-sorta be me. As he continued telling me his life story, I was astonished when he told me he was an elected politician from Kansas City, Kansas, almost falling off a bar stool in mid-afternoon. Wow.

Can someone explain to me how an elected politician could appear in public in such a state? Did he get reelected or resign in disgrace? He never told me his name; for all I know, it may have been Harvey Wallbanger or Captain Morgan. Can any of my readers who lived in KC in 1985 help me out?

Lessons learned:

- Everyone has a story, some of which are more interesting than others.

- Too bad smartphones didn't exist back then; I could have supplied recorded evidence to compel him to resign in disgrace. On the other hand, I'm far to kind to do that.

Billy the Kid

In spite of it being located in Texas, Arlington Stadium--home of the Texas Rangers--was cute. Although I didn't know it at the time, it was originally built as a small-capacity minor league ballpark. It had been expanded over the years, but still retained its charm. No concrete behemoth in Arlington! So much for the cliche that everything in Texas is big, although I found that to be true more often than not.

I am a New York Yankees hater. However, I was thrilled that Billy Martin was returning that night as their manager, yet another stint with the team.

In a sport that has its share of characters, Billy was in a class by himself. He and George Steinbrenner, the team owner, had a rather, um, mercurial relationship. Although George fired Billy five — five!--times, he just couldn't quit him. It was an ongoing saga, and Billy's unorthodox management style made for entertaining baseball.

Although the game started very badly, one of the Rangers ultimately hit three home runs and the team came from behind to win. Even though most fans largely seemed more interested in the beer and nachos, they were ecstatic at the victory.

My friend Charlie declined to attend the game because he is not a baseball fan. However, when I told him about it, he expressed his regrets that he didn't join me. After all, he belatedly realized, I was so much fun! He could have simply stuffed himself with ballpark food and listen to my witty color commentary.

OMG, the Rangers lost 99 games in 1985, but at least they won on my night. And they beat the effing Yankees.

Lesson learned: Let's savor our victories when we have them. Billy absolutely deserves his place in the Baseball Hall of Fame, and I'm sorry he died on Christmas.

Good Morning Baltimore

Because Baltimore had baseball, I had to go there. On the bus into town, a man named Louis struck up a conversation with me. Again, completely PG. However, he kept asking me when I would "move to Baltimore." Why would I want to do that? Baltimore was a boring, beige place in 1985. And Louis was a boring, beige person.

But I remember him. He even gave me his phone number, which caused me to laugh in disbelief after we parted ways.

Of course, Memorial Stadium was a concrete behemoth. Because I happened to attend on Mother's Day, all women received single carnations upon entrance. After waving them for the TV cameras, we were instructed to "OKAY, TAKE DOWN YOUR FLOWERS!" No, I've never heard that phrase since.

Orioles fans cracked themselves up; they were definitely one of the more amusing groups I witnessed. During the National Anthem, everyone shouted "O!" when "Oh say can you see" was sung. "O!" Orioles? Get it?

In addition, they loved to create rhyming little chants for the entertainment of themselves and the players. "Hey Dan, hit it to Japan!" "Hey Dauer, show us some power!" "Hey Rich, hit the son-of-a-b*tch!"

Fast forward to 2014. Camden Yards is much nicer than Memorial Stadium. Even though it is a large ballpark, it seemed intimate. Because the ticket prices weren't awful, we were so there.

Lots of impressive player statues, even though the team hasn't won the World Series since 1983. Also had some quality time with extended family and some reasonably good ballpark food. My most vivid memory, though, is of baseball fans having to share the parking garage with those attending the Comic-Con gathering at the Baltimore Convention Center next door.

When the game was over, my husband was searching for our car while gabbing with a male Comic-Con attendee wearing no shirt and a sparkly skirt. As a bonus visual, the guy was carrying a pretend sword. At least, I hope it was pretend.

As I watched them, I just had to marvel at two men strolling along and ignoring the different worlds they inhabited. It was very sweet.

Lessons learned:

- Louis, you were pleasant enough, but I had absolutely no intention of moving to Baltimore.

- I could only wave my Mother's Day carnation until it became irritating, but the intentions were good.

- People are nice when we can set aside our assumptions and differences, even — or especially — if they are dressed in edgy costumes. My husband still fondly remembers gabbing with the guy in the crazy costume as if he were his cubicle mate at the office.

City of Brotherly Love?

Philadelphia's Veterans' Stadium ballpark was another concrete behemoth. But because it was a ballpark I hadn't visited, I had to go there. They also displayed one of the funniest potato chip ads of all time: "Herr's is better than theirs." Yes, Herr's is the brand name; the person who created this ad deserves a place in the Advertising Hall of Fame.

Phillies fans are unrelenting (euphemism much?). The day before I arrived, Mike Schmidt, an infielder, commented that Phillies fans were "beyond help" and that apparently they didn't bow down to his superior talent. The next day, the boo-birds arrived ready to humiliate him and send him sobbing into the dugout.

His response was hilarious. He jogged to his position fully disguised in dark sunglasses and a dreadlock wig. Even the hateful fans had to laugh.

When I was leaving town, I stopped in for a good-enough dinner at a restaurant near the bus station. My waiter loved my "World Champions 1908 Chicago Cubs" T-shirt. After we gabbed a bit about the futility of the team at the time, he said he wanted that T-shirt. I told him that if he gave me the money, I would buy him the same T-shirt the next time I was at Wrigley. He did and I did.

Lessons learned:

- Never miss a chance to be kind. John, I hope you were pleasantly surprised when you received the T-shirt you paid me for.
- Phillies fans are brutal. Our family saw them play the Washington Nationals 25 years later. They never change, so be prepared.

The House That Ruth Built

Unless you are a Yankees fan, you hate the Yankees. However, I wanted to see and experience the House That Ruth Built. This phrase is a reference to Babe Ruth, a Hall of Fame player the Boston Red Sox traded, allegedly beginning the Curse of the Bambino, which took the Red Sox 86 years to overcome before they finally won another World Series.

I hate the Yankees as much as the next non-Yankees fan, but hopefully I would see them lose. I hopped on the subway and went to the Bronx, clenching my backpack all the way and keeping my cash stash in the money belt hidden under my T-shirt. Bahaha muggers, you will have to rip my shirt off in order to rob me…that is, if you notice the money belt under my baggy T-shirt or think that a starving student has enough money to risk an attempted robbery charge. But still, time for the badass walk. Just in case. And it was a day game; I couldn't afford to stay in New York City unless I was willing to deal with the hostels. Which I was not.

The neighborhood was nowhere nearly as fearful as I expected. After all, it was full of Yankee fans, not people seeking to rob me, rape me, or both. All good…as long as I pretended to be a Yankees fan.

The Yankees have a new stadium now, but I really enjoyed the original one. In particular, Monument Park, which was located behind center field, was fascinating.

When Monument Park was originally created in 1932, the inaugural monument was located in actual center field?! Center fielders had to dodge statues for over 40 years?! Thankfully, cooler heads prevailed; in the 1970s, the Yankees moved in the center field fence to ensure the angry center fielders would shut up. (A shorter distance required to hit a home run was an added bonus.)

I didn't realize it at the time, but Monument Park was not open to the public until 1985. I unintentionally timed my visit so that I could experience it firsthand. I love serendipity.

Because the Yankees have retired so many uniform numbers (too many great players, sigh), 0 is the only single-digit number available to their current players. And those players' accomplishments were on display in Monument Park. I even stopped hating them for a minute there.

Lesson learned: I never knew where I would find really great museums. Monument Park is still featured at the new stadium. Even though I'm sure it is similarly great and awe-inspiring, I am still allowed to hate the Yankees. Except for Aaron Judge; I hear he's a really nice guy.

Meet the Mets

I cannot pretend I attended Billy Joel's concert at Shea Stadium in 2011, which is now replaced by Citi Field. But I can attest to seeing the adorable Home Run Apple, which the organization relocated to the new stadium.

I was not a big Mets fan when I went to Shea; it was just a list item to check off. But the Home Run Apple...how cute is that? When a Mets player hits a home run, the apple jumps up and celebrates along with the fans.

In subsequent years, ballparks have implemented celebratory gestures after the home team scores. A mascot taking a trip down a slide. Players waiting in the dugout sporting beaded necklaces. Swords. Hats shaped like cheese wedges (I am not making this up). That said, the Home Run Apple was in a class by itself at the time. Thankfully, the Mets hit a couple of home runs; it was a kick to see it in action.

Lesson learned: I, cynic that I was and am, could be impressed by a silly prop.

Sweet Caroline and Dirty Water

Off to see the Boston Red Sox at Fenway Park, which is a baseball fan's pilgrimage site.

(Full disclosure: In the 1980s, the stadium didn't actually play the songs referenced in this vignette title, but I am confident I can get it past my readers who are not Red Sox fans.)

Fenway was such a great place in the 1980s. In subsequent years, I told friends they simply had to go to the Cask 'n Flagon, which at the time was a hole in the wall with a lot of Red Sox memorabilia and very entertaining fans with whom to gab. Unfortunately, I did not realize it had moved to a new, larger location and transformed itself into a neon bar. Sigh. But let's focus on the better years.

I had time before the game to soak up the ambiance. Gabbed with some guys from New Hampshire at the Cask 'n Flagon. I suppose there were no female baseball fans in their state because while we engaged in the requisite how-bout-those-Sox banter, one of the guys kept exclaiming, "WHAT A WOMAN! WHAT A WOMAN!" All of them were gentlemen, and after parting, I walked off to find my seat while marveling as to what a woman I might be.

There was much to admire about the venue and the fans.

- A Fenway Frank is served in the cutest hot dog bun ever. The dog itself is supposedly a great and unique recipe. Maybe not 11 herbs and spices, analogous to the formerly good KFC chicken, but still unique. And the buns! They are basically folded pieces of bread; they look nothing like a garden variety hot dog bun. So. Adorable.

- Kool-Aid, "America's relief pitcher," threw out the first pitch. It was an homage to a silly TV ad from the 1980s, but it was cute and amusing.

- The fans really know their team and really know the game. They focus on who stinks and who doesn't. And they were happy to remind the players of their opinions. With minimal potty mouth.

For better or worse, Red Sox fans never forget. Years later, they remember the pitcher who gave up the home run that sent the Yankees to the 1978 World Series (Mike Torrez). Years later, they happily remember the home run that sent them to the 1986 World Series (Dave Henderson). Years later, they remember the first baseman who made a horrible gaffe that led to a 1986 World Series choke (Bill Buckner). Yes, it was awful. Poor Bill; he actually had to move away from New England.

Lesson learned: Fenway Park was better Back in the Day. I know that makes me sound old.

Thnks Fr th Mmrs

Fast backward to 1980. You theoretically asked me (back in FAQs) about my most memorable experiences. This is one of them.

On June 27, I and my first real love went to a Giants vs. Dodgers game at the late, not-lamented, horribly cold Candlestick Park. I was seeing somebody else at the time, but when what's-his-name agreed to go the game with me, I immediately dropped the other what's-his-name and cleared my schedule.

In the previous two years, we hung out a lot, gabbed a lot, listened to music a lot. He had dropped out of school and meanwhile, I was headed for college. He does not qualify as a Bad Boyfriend because he was never my boyfriend, but insisted he would love me some day. And I believed it. Promises, promises.

We arrive at the game and moderately exchanged goo-goo eyes throughout. I had waited for this date for waaay too long, and I thought this was the night he would finally confess that he loved me. Bahaha.

Back to the game. I was excited to be spending the evening on a kinda-sorta date, but experienced an unexpected surprise. The Dodgers' pitcher, Jerry Reuss, threw a no-hitter, which only occurred once that season over more than 2000 games.

Giants vs. Dodgers is a not-so-friendly rivalry. In the final inning of the game, picture a stadium full of Giants fans cheering on a Dodger, comparable to MAGA Republicans cheering on a Democrat. It was that strange, but awesome. Not many fans can witness a no-hitter, and I am thankful I am one of the few and the proud who have.

Lessons learned:

- I would never forget my first and only no-hitter. Glad I was able to experience one in person.
- I would never forget my first love. Even though I'm happily married, I hope I run into him someday before either of us dies. Hey, it could happen.

PART FOUR

Pride is good, but sometimes it makes me do some real dumb stuff. I know I can survive this trip, but am quite lonesome. At least when I traveled in my nation, I could visit people; here, I can't. None of the guidebooks mention culture shock. My favorite part of my personality—sarcasm—is impossible here.

--Journal entry, September 1, 1985

The Wrong Thing to Do

"Everyone has a great idea that will not work."

Although I may be implying that a wiser person said this before me, I cannot find a source. Damn you, internet; I really tried to find the wiser person.

Similar quotes are attributed to Jack Dorsey and Nolan Bushnell, but theirs aren't this one. I may have read it in a Letter to the Editor (ask your elders), but this line doesn't even strike a bell with my husband. Therefore, I guess I can claim it for my own? If anyone can identify the original source of this line, I will attribute in my second printing. If I have one.

In the meantime, let's revel in the stupid decisions I fortunately survived. Self-deprecation is fun after I survived said decisions.

There were only a handful of decisions that could have killed me; obviously, none of them did. Only one could have landed me in prison, but we won't go there. Bad Boyfriends, sigh.

On the Boardwalk, Not Under It

I arrived in Atlantic City only to be faced with ridiculous hotel prices. Having spent time at Nevada casinos, I assumed the casino hotels would be similarly cheap in order to lure me to their blackjack tables and slot machines, but nooo…damn you, Donald Trump! He owned several casinos and apparently thought offering $39 hotel rooms and $1.99 breakfasts was too hard.

Found a zero-star hotel with no private bath and a loud bar located beneath my room, but no worries. Checked in, all good, time to explore.

I went for a swim in the Atlantic Ocean. So. Gosh. Darn. Cold. But refreshing, I guess. After that, I walked on the boardwalk barefoot. Who does that? The first day of my trip and I ripped open my foot by stepping on a nail.

Thankfully, there was an emergency room within walking distance. Somehow I managed to limp over, where I got a tetanus shot and a serious scolding from a nurse that asked me how I could be such an idiot. I had no answer.

God bless the person who invented gauze and adhesive tape. Because of those two items, I was able to live with my wound and continue to travel. That said, what the heck was I thinking? Oh yeah, I wasn't.

Lessons learned:

- Duh. Don't walk barefoot on a boardwalk.
- Given the chance, Donald Trump will always gouge his customers.

The Hard Way

I found myself in a small town in Pennsylvania. Arrived there by train rather than bus. I had heard about the beautiful foliage in that part of our nation, and was dumbstruck by the view outside my window. It was such a happy surprise to randomly encounter such scenic rides.

I disembarked from the train and needed to walk to my motel. Stupidly, I noticed a railroad bridge. "Hey, look! A shortcut!" Because I always looked forward to the nights I could sleep in an actual bed rather on a large vehicle in motion, I wanted to arrive ASAP. And it looked like a short walk until I started to cross it.

Big mistake. Huge. Although I obviously made it across the bridge, it scared me to death.. Don't look down. Don't look down. Don't fall into that river below. Or, to address more mundane concerns, don't let my backpack fall into that river. Even if it didn't get swept away, is there a laundromat in this postage stamp of a town?

To this day, I continue to be fearful of railroad bridges. I walk daily in a state park five minutes from my home. Bicyclists regularly ride across its short railroad bridge. Me? I walk three steps, look down, and flee in horror.

Lesson learned: Shortcuts were not a good idea if they made me fear for my life.

It's Always Sunny in Philadelphia...Unfortunately

Not a hostel girl, but I had to make an exception in pricey Philadelphia. There was a cheap hostel in Fairmount Park that was a reasonably simple bus ride from downtown. I arrived at dusk and the fireflies were just beginning their nightly display, which is very entertaining. Bugs that actually light up at dusk? Who thought of this? Oh yeah...God.

The hostel didn't need no stinking bedrooms. Instead, there was one stinking—in the literal sense—sleeping room. No air conditioning. So. Gosh. Darn. Hot.

I'm sure that wasn't my most uncomfortable night, but it was certainly in the top three. How on earth was I supposed to sleep in a sweaty room full of sweaty strangers? It made me long for a night on the bus. Do I dare shower? I don't think I did, because ewww. How long had it been since that shower had actually been cleaned? If I didn't shower, who would notice the stink that emanated from me in comparison with the general stink of them room? My prepared, but unnecessary response: "It's not me, it's you!"

During my hours of insomnia, my dominant thought was that tomorrow had better be fun, and the cheesesteak had better be as good as it is reputed to be. Thankfully, it was. I don't think I ate at the reputedly best cheesesteak joint in town, but my tummy was happy and so was my wallet.

Lesson learned: Tough times don't last, but tough people do. Not really…the real lesson is that some hostels just plain suck.

Saving Grace

Apparently due to an act of God, I managed to book an advance reservation for a dorm room at the University of Chicago. Reasonably good and very affordable, but what an adventure to get there.

The subway map indicated I should travel to a particular station. Apparently, there are easier ways to get there now. After nearly forty years, things change. Imagine that.

When the train reached the end of the line, I was dropped off in a horrible neighborhood and was genuinely afraid. Aside from that, I was wearing short shorts and a tank top. (Geez, it was a hot day. Is that so wrong?) "Hey everyone, I'm a young woman traveling alone. Come on over, rob me or rape me. Your call."

Then, a super-sweet man named Jerome sensed my discomfort and volunteered to escort me to my destination. Ironically, the super-sweet man was nicer than the dorm residents were.

The residents weren't outright mean, but were obviously in another world, even though I was only a year out of college. However, their parents were spending a lot more on tuition than my parents ever did; maybe it was the economic divide.

Although my room was good enough, I wasn't interested in socializing with the students, even though I probably could have if I were so inclined. But, you know, the lone wolf thing.

Instead, I walked to the nearby commons in the evening. Because it was abuzz with students, I felt safe. Instead of talking to people, I brought my Walkman (remember what that is?), listened to Tom Petty's live album, and sang along. Live albums were a thing back then, and this one was four—count 'em, four--sides. That was a lot of great music even if you don't know what "sides" means.

It was summer; I wouldn't freeze to death as I would in winter. I didn't need to attempt making fast friends who believed they were too good for me. I had places to go, people to meet, and things to see.

Lessons learned:

- Jim Croce was wrong; the south side of Chicago is not the baddest part of town.

- Geez, Toni, know your route. I quickly learned of an express bus that would literally drop me off at the university itself. And used it for the remainder of my stay.

Zero From Outer Space

I was at a bus stopover in Jackson, Mississippi, dressed in my usual traveling clothes: T-shirt, sweatshirt, sweat pants. My late brother-in-law was consistently bemused by how I dressed, but he always thought I dressed like crap. Guilty as charged, but one word: comfort. More words: the less I spent on clothes, the more I could spend on more important and memorable experiences.

I did not understand why people stared at me as if I had boogers coming out of my nose. Was it obvious that I was an evil Californian? Okay, I can accept that I did not look like a local. But still. Some people need to be suspicious of whom they perceive to be outsiders. But I was just walking and stretching my legs; I don't think that was wrong.

I am thankful to report that this was the only place I felt so judged. But gosh, someone could have said hello and we could have engaged in some witty repartee. However, they preferred to focus on the proverbial boogers coming out of my nose.

Lesson learned: We are all in search of human contact, or just a laugh, a smile, or a how-bout-those-fill-in-name-of-team conversation. Even if I wasn't familiar with the team being discussed, I could pretend I was. Or at least ask my temporary friends why they were a fan of what's-his-face.

Not Raised by Wolves…No, Really

Fast forward to 2012. Chicago is pleasant in the summer. On most days, shorts are doable, in contrast to the brutal winters during which people—let's face it, guys—would provide competing narratives regarding how few layers they require in December. Okay guys, have fun with that.

Over the years, I have been impressed that the city's vibe isn't all about sports, although it's undeniably a big sports town. Chicago holds art dear, and public art is conveniently available for viewing. And we're not just talking about artists who were unable to quit their day jobs. Alexander Calder, Marc Chagall, Joan Miro, Keith Haring, even more. Outside. For free.

Continuing the public art theme, Millennium Park presents my favorite type of concerts (free) during summer months. Classical music? Why not? At least it wouldn't destroy my hearing, as my preferred live music shows will probably do. Eventually.

At the urging of our middle offspring, we attended a classical performance and were thoroughly enchanted by the refreshing change of pace. No F-words! No musicians in tasteless outfits! Just pretty and relaxing music. But then things went south.

Stupid us #1: We thought we were supposed to applaud after each beautiful song, but no: we needed to wait until each "movement" was performed. We figured that out pretty quickly, after realizing we were the only idiots applauding.

Stupid us #2: My husband and I thought we were allowed to whisper "isn't this awesome" to one another during the performance, but nooo. A woman sitting in front of us channeled her inner disciplinary Catholic school teacher: "SHHHHHHHH!" She probably shushed us louder than we were whispering. And her evil eye provided a bonus level of attempted humiliation.

Okay, Mother Superior, we will behave. But we just wanted to broaden our cultural horizons. Is that so wrong?

As the concert approached its end, a horribly subversive thought surfaced. What if I decided to shout "FREEBIRD" before the last song? (Ask your elders.) Surely that would crack someone up. After all, it was a free concert; surely we weren't the only classical music newbies or the only ones who would get the joke. Ultimately, I decided not to do so.

Concert completed, on our way back to the hotel. When I shared my fleeting idea with my husband, I told him we probably would have been thrown out. His response: "No. *You* would have been thrown out."

Lessons not learned (even now):

- Why does the audience not applaud after every song at a classical concert?

- Why could we not whisper? Heck, we can whisper in church.

Bless Me Father, For I May Have Sinned

Confession, now known in the Catholic Church as Reconciliation, is by nature confidential. I don't need to tell you why I felt the need to receive this sacrament at New Orleans' St.

Louis Cathedral. Use your imagination, but don't get carried away; it wasn't that awful. It just involved going to the Dungeon, a French Quarter club that opened at midnight. Oooh, the intrigue! While many dance clubs get ready to wind down at midnight, the Dungeon was just getting started.

I didn't exit the club until the sun came up, then walked back to my hostel last looking only vaguely like an unhoused person. After using one of my all-you-can-eat breakfast coupons (thanks, Alabama brothers Robert and Dick), I slept. Thankfully, the hostel was open 24 hours a day, unlike some that enforce lockout hours during the day. But heck, New Orleans…only God knows when people would stroll or stumble in.

When I woke up, I felt like I had done something wrong. After all, what was a reasonably good Catholic girl doing dancing the night away in a club with vaguely satanic overtones? The music was great, I had a blast, and I didn't end up in a ditch. That said, I was off to the cathedral.

The priest was just sweet, and afterward, I couldn't help but wonder what confessions he had heard over the years. Being in the middle of the French Quarter, what types of sins were penitents likely to confess after they had one or two too many Hurricanes (an extremely potent cocktail, which I have never had)? Or on Ash Wednesday, the day after Mardi Gras?

We will never know. Priests aren't allowed to tell. But the kindness, love, and forgiveness I received from the priest was incredibly comforting.

Lesson learned: Thanks, Father Awesome. He made me realize there was nothing wrong with dancing while most people were sleeping…as long as only dancing was involved.

It's Raining Again

California girl that I am, I grew up so sheltered that I did not realize it rained in summer. I guess that's why real estate is cheaper almost everywhere except the Golden State. For the price we pay for real estate, the weather should be good, for crissakes.

After I had been traveling for a couple of months, I was astonished by the crappy weather my national neighbors routinely deal with. Sunny Memorial Day weekend? Bahaha.

I wanted to have fun on a holiday weekend, but it was awful in the Midwest. Can't I even go to a baseball game? No, they were all rained out. Sigh.

I tried to go to the Indianapolis 500. I'd previously only been to an auto race in which Sam Arena, one of Dad's friends, participated. It was loud, but I didn't exactly have a choice regarding whether to attend. I mean, I was an obedient daughter.

Good intentions aside, the Indianapolis weather was horrible, so I desperately researched alternate bus routes. I finally found a city with not-awful weather, then found a one-star room I could hide in. Actual blankets and guilty-pleasure TV are good. Having a place to hang my damp clothes was also good.

Lessons learned:

- Sunny California is not a figure of speech.

- I guess I wish I could have attended the Indy 500, but no regrets. It was probably too loud for my taste. And all that exhaust. Have fun with that.

Crawling Back to You

When in Miami, it is not a smart choice to stay in a zero-star room. I mean, a truly awful room, in which each wall was painted in a different color...I suppose, whatever leftover paint happened to be taking up space in the painter's garage.

I spent a very pleasant day in Miami Beach. The water in the south Atlantic is very warm, much better than the frigid water in some other locales. I greatly enjoyed my swim, and nobody stole my stuff that was unattended on shore. Go Miami!

When I checked into my motel, I immediately saw that I needed to barricade the door. Did I say immediately?

I was determined to relax in my every-third-night hotel room. However, as I settled down to watch some bad TV, my room started crawling. Really. The air conditioning malfunctioned and the tropical bug party started.

I was unable to contact the front desk because they probably locked us in and went the heck home. Instead, I moved my backpack to higher ground and resigned myself to the fact that I would just have to cross my fingers that the bugs wouldn't try to join me in bed. Spoiler alert: they didn't.

Lesson learned: I needed functional air conditioning in Florida, even if it would cost more. I also needed a suitable method of sending invasive bugs to an untimely death. I ended up carrying a paperback book, which I knew I would never read because of the bug corpses on its cover. At least I encased the book in a Ziploc bag to ensure the corpses wouldn't contaminate my intermittently clean clothes.

Wicked Game

Manhattan was crazy and overwhelming during my first visit. In the not-so-good old days, the subway was frightening and should have had a sign at each station: "Abandon hope all ye who enter here." Really awful. Pee smells. Graffiti. Ewww.

That said, I was happy to see the city's street performers. Among others, a group of women sang and danced to the Supremes' greatest hits; a group of men performed a comparable rendition of the Temptations' greatest hits. They were able to persuade spectators to join their dances. I declined, but the entire crowd was laughing and thoroughly entertained.

As I moved on, I unfortunately played three-card Monty with $20. Twenty dollars! I think I was the only person at the time who didn't realize what a sucker game it is, but basically the Guy Who Ran It showed three cards, shuffled them, placed them face down, and invited spectators to bet they could identify the location of a particular card. What could go wrong? Of course, I lost.

At that time, $20 was a huge amount of money. I was blindsided. I sulked as I walked away, feeling too stupid to live. But other people were playing, so it was moderately comforting to know I was not the only stupid person there. Unless they were wise to the tricks of the Guy Who Ran It.

Lesson learned: Toni, don't ever play three-card Monty again.

Down With the Sickness

Departing on a boat from Dover, UK, to the Continent. Met a couple of travelers, including one guy from New Jersey who almost ran over Bruce Springsteen while The Boss was attempting to cross a street. Dubious claim to fame, but a good story. Because Bruce is still alive, he obviously didn't hit him. Not sure when this happened, but thankfully he didn't ruin the chance of "Born in the USA" being released. What would Ronald Reagan have done? (Ask your elders.)

We were all gabbing while waiting to board our reasonably sized tourist boat. I was picturing a fun night of socializing, dancing, then collapsing peacefully into my economy seat. Bahaha!

The crossing to Calais was the most violent sea crossing I have ever experienced. Expecting a fun night, I instead spent the trip in my seat feeling horribly dizzy, praying I didn't vomit, and just wishing for it to be over. Dancing? Are you serious? I barely slept while ensuring a barf bag was at convenient distance. I should have taken Dramamine, but had no idea this trip would be so awful.

Lessons learned:

- Dramamine is my friend, especially because I am prone to motion sickness.
- Before taking a boat tour, ask the internet how brutal the sea is. The staff might minimize the conditions just to meet their ticket quota.

This Town is Looking Like a Ghost Town

I have established that I am Sicilian, and that my grandparents immigrated to our nation on the boats that arrived on Ellis Island.

Because of that, I simply had to visit the town of Nola (my maiden name), which is located a few minutes from Naples. Heritage, oh yeah. Photo ops, oh yeah. Relatives, maybe.

I departed the train, only to witness a godforsaken hellhole. Flies everywhere, just general squalor. The train conductor must have wondered to himself what on earth the stupid American girl was thinking. On the other hand, doubtful that he cared; he earned his paycheck regardless.

In hindsight, I should have ventured into the actual town. Maybe the train station was located on the proverbial wrong side of the tracks. Nola has a fairly fascinating history, but I was scared off by the squalor that "greeted" me.

Who knew that St. Paulinus hailed from Nola, and that he was credited with introducing bells into Catholic Masses? Who knew who St. Paulinus was? Furthermore, who knew that Nola also had a bunch of artifacts buried by an eruption of Mt. Vesuvius? Take that, Pompeii! Why should you get all of the publicity?

Fast forward to 2013. Our family ate ridiculously great pizza at Naples' Pizzeria di Matteo. (Former President Bill Clinton ate there! They have pictures and everything!) We spontaneously noticed that the appellation of our wine was Nola. Of course, that made me feel even more stupid and judgmental when remembering my twentysomething actions when I fled the town. Probably a lot of history and some good wine. But I let the flies at the train station scare me off.

Lesson learned: Before dismissing a town, find out what happened there. I was too young and dumb to research a town that shared my original surname, but I could have ignored the flies and instead bragged to residents that "my name is Nola too."

No Jokes Allowed

Contrary to the narrative I am trying to convey, I am not always happy, silly, and optimistic.

Trying to present my travels in a mostly deadpan and humorous manner, which is mostly how I remember them. That said, this chapter recalls some sad places.

My adventures are not all happy talk, even though it's more fun to focus on the silly. Who would want to read a memoir about how much life stinks? Not sure, but I think Pete Townshend tried. And Tom Petty's life surely stunk at some points.

Let's agree that nobody's life is perfect, and certainly not a nonstop parade of Facebook humble-bragging posts about how "blessed" we are. I really want to quote a Tom Petty lyric I regularly repeat to myself and my kids, but would have to pay money to do so. At this point, I am almost willing to spend the money because it's such a great song. (Hint: search for the first lines of the lyrics to "Walls.")

I mostly continue laughing, but once in a while, I and you may tear up. Nothing wrong with that. My life has overall been great, but I don't want to pretend I didn't have rough times. Somehow, most of us get through, but not all. Miss you, Rich.

That said, let's resume laughing after this chapter and after this book…as often as possible.

I'm So Afraid, and Also Appalled

As a California girl who grew up in a White neighborhood, I feel alternatively grateful and embarrassed that I had not witnessed the ugly underbelly of outright racism. However, when I did…wow. This dumb 22-year-old thought racism was a thing of the past. And I had no idea that in our not-so-distant past, lynchings were so common that they were routinely featured in newspapers, often reported next to graduation announcements and stock prices. But back to tourism.

I felt I needed to go to Disney World because it is theoretically the happiest place on earth. I headed to Orlando, but whatever. On the other hand, I'm really not an amusement park girl, so I guess it was me, not the mouse. That said, I had two experiences in Orlando that were awful. The first one scared me and the second one appalled me.

- Scary: I was walking back to my zero-star room. Because it was a Sunday night, all the downtown businesses were closed. As I proceeded, I noticed that two men were following me in their car and I was very frightened. I had carried tear gas, but this was the first time I had it in my hand ready to use. After I fearfully approached the car of a hopefully kind elderly couple, they drove me back to my room. It all worked out and I didn't die.

- Appalling: At the Orlando Greyhound station, I was thirsty. These were the days in which we didn't constantly carry bottles of water as if we were about to traverse the Sahara Desert. As I approached the drinking fountain, a Black woman was ahead of me, and she deferred to me. Why? I don't remember if I assured the woman to use the fountain first or if I was too shocked to respond. But wow, it was weird.

Lessons learned:

- If I feel unsafe enough to have tear gas at the ready, take a gosh-darn taxi.
- Somehow the right people appeared at the right time.
- Racism is ugly. I and the Black woman were thirsty. Why could I cut in line?

Never Again?

Dachau, located in Munich, was one of many Nazi-era concentration camps. I am thankful I experienced it, but what an awful place.

Thankfully, there were no human tour guides giving awkward tours, and rightly so. I and my fellow visitors were able to simply wander the grounds and imagine the horrors that took place there.

The route included the dorms and bunk beds the Holocaust victims slept in before their demise. The seemingly benign street gutters actually drained the blood flow of the murdered. WTF?

And the photos. Emaciated people. People who may have been my friends if they lived down the street from me.

Many others were visiting, but the haunting aspect is that it was very, very, very quiet. Hard to discuss lunch plans while witnessing a place of such shocking brutality.

Dachau does not describe personal stories of those who were incarcerated there, but I found one on my own. Titus Brandsma, a

Catholic saint, vehemently resisted the Nazi occupation; he was arrested and sent to Dachau. He was supportive of his fellow prisoners, but ultimately died as a result of a medical experiment other prisoners experienced. Because of his faith, he gave a wooden rosary to the nurse who administered his fatal injection and calmly encouraged her to change her ways. She ultimately became Catholic and testified to his holiness.

Some Catholic saints are amazing. Even if you aren't Catholic, read about them occasionally. Some of them did crazy-good things, and most of them did not suffer a horrible martyr-ish death. Although Titus Brandsma certainly did.

Lesson learned: I will defer to the sign posted in several languages at the entrance: "Never Again."

Hard For Us to Say We're Sorry, But We Are

The human brain is a wondrous miracle. I arrived in Nuremberg, West Germany, a couple of weeks after recovering from my Dachau shock. Exhausted, I fell asleep while listening to music in my zero-star room. At least I was in a room and not on public transit.

When a Tom Petty song played, I woke up. And that's not even the first time that happened with Tom's songs. For that reason, I reassured myself. "Positive, positive, positive! Today is going to be a good day!"

I'm still baffled as to why I spent so much time in West Germany because Italy was much better. But here I was in Nuremberg. Surprised at how sad it really was. Dachau wasn't depressing enough, I suppose.

Of course, I completely understand why the residents needed to apologize for the Holocaust. Throughout my time in West Germany, it was very sad to witness how many men were permanently disabled due to their injuries during World War II and—I assume--the reign of the Nazis. As an American girl, I never recall routinely encountering disabled men in our nation. I wish I would have engaged some of the German injured; most of them probably spoke English.

But Nuremberg. I did a couple of tours there and the overriding theme was, "WE'RE SORRY! WE ARE! WHAT ON EARTH WERE WE THINKING?" Yes, the capitalization emphasis is necessary.

Okay, I get it. The residents were very ashamed of their nation's history, and rightly so. I was probably too young and naive to know the children realized their parents were honestly trying to acknowledge the shame that was their nation's history.

Perhaps it was too much for me to take, and it was easier to say in my twentysomething mind, "Can you just shut up already?"

Lesson (eventually) learned: Even though I was too stupid at the time to understand why Germans were repeatedly compelled to apologize for the Holocaust, I finally got it. And Holocaust deniers, really? For a different reason, I need to repeat my initial ignorant Nuremberg reaction to the present-day Holocaust deniers: "Can you just shut up already?"

I Think I'm in Troubles

Belfast, Northern Ireland--sometimes known as Ulster--is a beautiful city. Its residents were friendly and definitely had the gift of gab. That said, it was a sad and poignant experience to witness the ongoing Troubles firsthand.

The Troubles were frequently characterized as Catholics versus Protestants, but they can also be characterized as a battle between Irish Nationalists wanting to unite with the Irish Republic, versus Unionists wanting to remain a part of the United Kingdom. Do your own research and form your own opinion. At any rate, it was sobering, even though I never felt in personal danger.

I checked into a reasonably nice hotel. It didn't give me pause to have to go through a metal detector to enter. However, according to one of my Belfast fast friends, I learned the running joke: "Why did the owners change the name of the Europa Hotel? So the Irish Republican Army (IRA) couldn't find it."

Unbeknownst to me when I decided to stay there, the Forum Hotel was known as the most-bombed hotel in the world after experiencing 36 bombings by the IRA. Thankfully, no lives were lost; obviously, not mine.

Probably due to my oblivion, I really enjoyed my stay. Their full Irish breakfasts were amazing. Broiled (or maybe fried or maybe roasted) tomatoes as a side dish. Yes, I am embarrassed that my appetite temporarily took precedence over the ongoing events in Belfast.

Strolled casually around downtown on a Saturday afternoon. All of a sudden, bomb threats, stores closed, people evacuated. Then I heard music.

My visit coincided with "marching season," during which the Unionist Orange Order—a fraternity whose purpose was to maintain Ulster's association with the United Kingdom—marched down the streets to remind the Irish Nationalists that they prevailed and the Irish Nationalists lost. The Unionists insist their marches are a celebration, but it seemed rather passive-aggressive to outsider me. Very haunting. And the music echoed and echoed. And echoed.

I did a bus tour of Belfast and was astonished at how fortified the police stations were. Razor wire. Security fences. I was also astonished that the obituary pages of the newspaper were two full pages long. Every day I was there.

When I was gabbing with my newfound friends, I asked how the two sides knew who was whom. After all, it wasn't a visual distinction such as skin color. They responded that it was their neighborhood and, to a lesser extent, their last name. In retrospect, I can't help but wonder if I "looked Catholic." I had no idea Catholics looked a certain way, but maybe? My (minimal) makeup? My (thrift-shop) fashion? Why were none of my fast friends Protestant? Or was it just the part of town I was in?

I had a wonderful time In Belfast, but OMG it was sad. IMO, the religious aspect was not the main problem; it was the nationalistic aspect. As you know by now, I am a cradle Catholic and the last time I checked, my priests were not encouraging their congregations to bomb and shoot others who practiced other religious traditions.

The 1998 Good Friday Agreement kinda-sorta ended The Troubles. Kind-sorta.

Lesson learned: I'm still trying to figure that out. But I am thankful I was able to experience it, albeit from a tourist distance. And I recently read a very poignant quote from Roma Downey: "My mother never got a chance to use her wedding china. It was locked in a little cabinet. When the Troubles escalated, a tank rumbled down the street and all the china broke. Live like each day is your last." Maybe that's the lesson.

Formerly a Nation of Enemies

Fast forward to 2014. Our wonderful daughter married a wonderful Chilean. Because of that, I had the opportunity to moderately experience the aftermath of the Chilean dictatorship, which lasted from 1973 until 1990.

I was able to visit Chile twice. A looong flight, and I'm not getting any younger. But while I was there, I was able to learn about a truly horrible time.

Salvador Allende was a socialist politician who was lawfully elected as Chile's president in 1970. However, to say the least, he angered many.

On September 11, 1973, he was the target of a military coup with the support of our nation's government. It is alleged that Allende committed suicide during the attack, but some dispute that. Regardless, he died, and here comes Augusto Pinochet. He recruited the American-based Chicago Boys--of course they were American...I mean, duh--to slap Chile into capitalist shape.

I do realize that many Americans recognize South America as a thing, but don't comprehend the impact of the dictatorship. Truth be told, I did not know myself until our family's newfound Chile connection motivated me to do some reading. Not judging, just attempting to educate.

Depending on the Chilean, the dictatorship was either an "unfortunate but necessary era" or a truly awful time. I vote for the awful. Although I only speak *poquito Espanol*, I was able to sense when an elderly Chilean family member was defending that era because a strange vibe descended over the dinner table while he was talking. Don't argue with Grandpa; let's just let him vent. I guess.

How could I say "I don't think so" in Spanish? And did a woke American really have the right to weigh in on the struggles of a South American nation, the struggles of which I learned only because our daughter fell in love with one of their citizens? And— full disclosure—I didn't know what Grandpa was actually saying. But the vibe.

La Moneda, located in Santiago, is comparable to our nation's White House. Although the tour had its moments—we were able to pretend we were giving speeches from the president's podium—the tour guide had to acknowledge the events of 1973. Our guide pointed out the door through which Allende's dead body was removed, and indicated that nobody would use that door for many, many years. He didn't indicate whether he was or wasn't a *Pinochetista* (Pinochet supporter), but he moderately addressed the issue and I appreciated that.

At the time, the palace did not officially recognize Pinochet with a commemorative medal or some other bling, as was the case for all his predecessors who did not incarcerate and torture their citizens. I hope that has not changed, but the internet cannot confirm one way or the other.

After a much-needed lunch break, we were off to the Museum of Memory and Human Rights, also in Santiago. Continuing to remedy my American oblivion, it was astonishing to see how many people suffered under Pinochet. My bilingual daughter and Spanish-speaking son-in-law spoke with a woman whose brother had disappeared and was never found. And the photos of all the others...I was speechless. These people had mothers, fathers, probably siblings, maybe kids. And they disappeared.

We continued to Concepcion, our daughter's home at the time, a political hotspot that could arguably be characterized as the nation's most progressive city. Contrary to possible belief, Chile is not a third-world country. And OMG, the *torta de amor* is the second-best dessert on the planet. Maybe there is a better one, but I'm not recalling any right now. Why aren't Americans baking this? Thankfully, I have a recipe, so take that!

Back to the no-jokes-allowed stuff.

Because I walk in my nearby state park every day, I took walks through downtown Concepcion just to maintain my kinda-sorta fitness regimen. Although it is just another large city for the most part, some of it surprised me.

There are many schools in its downtown. My son-in-law informed me that one of them housed prisoners—the "domestic terrorists," I guess—during the Pinochet era. And yes, some prisoners were tortured.

During my benign walk to the grocery store, a group of uniformed high school students were protesting something. Because of the language barrier thing, I didn't know why they were protesting. All I knew was that a bunch of teenagers were mad about something and were peacefully trying to explain.

"Thanks" to the Pinochet era, protesters would sometimes be confronted by *guanacos*—vehicles named after a relative of spitting llamas. The term became a colloquialism for the police vehicles who forcefully fired water on those who dared protest. But these were kids. In school uniforms. Why on earth were the *guanacos* ready and waiting? In fairness, the *carabineros* (police) did not use them. But IMO, the intimidation factor was not necessary. I wish I could say that the *guanacos* have been retired, but no.

Chile is a beautiful country and I am so glad I was able to see it. But geez, it seems as if there was always an undercurrent of tension. I'm truly glad my daughter's family doesn't live there anymore because it seemed like hell could spontaneously break loose at any minute. On the other hand, I was only there for two weeks. What did I know?

And BTW, the title of this vignette is a shoutout to a great, informative, and balanced book: "A Nation of Enemies." Pamela Constable rocks. Read it and cry about the deaths of Victor Jara and Pablo Neruda. I know I did.

Lesson learned: South America has had some brutal moments in its history. In addition to Chile, there was Brazil, Argentina, and Uruguay. Although I loved Chile, I couldn't help but wonder if a seemingly normal city could descend into chaos at the drop of a hat. Think it can't happen in our nation? I hope not.

What's So Funny About Peace, Love, and Understanding?

Fast forward to 2019. Yes, this chapter deserves two fast forwards.

I and my husband were enjoying our first extended trip with just the two of us. We happily anticipated Memphis minor league baseball, the legendary Sun Studios, and some great entertainment in a musically awesome city. We also anticipated visiting the Lorraine Motel museum, located at the site where Martin Luther King Jr. was assassinated.

Woke snowflakes (or not), do you want to see a museum or what? The Lorraine Motel will stay with you forever. In general, my museum shelf life is two or three hours. However, the National Civil Rights Museum at the Lorraine Motel (its official name) left me speechless. Because I was speechless, I can only attempt my written commentary.

I was only six years old when MLK was shot and killed, but strangely enough, I remember it as something that was awful and tragic. Why my parents didn't turn off the TV, I will never know. Perhaps they were too busy arguing.

The museum recreates the struggles of our Black brothers and sisters who, quite literally, risked their lives in their efforts to secure their civil rights, allegedly granted by our Constitution. And the museum's curators have recreated the actual state of MLK's room—including the coffee cups and semi-filled ashtrays—when he was assassinated.

The compelling manner the museum presents our Black brothers' and sisters' struggles is sobering. Although I am lucky to last in a museum for two hours, I and my husband were there all day. We left in tears...I did, anyway. My husband doesn't cry.

Go to it. Experience for yourself the renderings of the anguished shouts of the enslaved. Experience the bravery of the Montgomery bus boycott, the Freedom Riders, and the numerous others who literally risked—and sometimes lost—their lives in the cause of freedom. Learn about Claudette Colvin, a 15-year-old who refused to surrender her seat on the bus nine months before Rosa Parks did likewise. Admire the bravery of all.

And cringe.

Don't get me wrong; I am proud to be an American. But gosh, we have plenty to be ashamed of. I mean, the "Negro Motorist Green Book" was a travel guide published for over 30 years to help our Black citizens safely travel the county during a time of rampant segregation and prejudice. Really? Really? Really?

Lesson learned: The truth hurts. That said, I bow to those willing to tell it, even if too many of our actual snowflake leaders want to shield the kids from our deplorable history.

I'm On My Way

My trips weren't over until they were over. Join me as I am alternatively tired, road-weary, scared, sleeping on buses and in airport terminals, and meeting great people as I moved closer to making my way back to the left coast.

Down But It Won't Last Long

Traveling alone. Meeting random people most days. Not forging relationships (but hi again Darryl in Chicago). But didn't I get lonely?

Short answer: Yes. And no.

Of course, traveling alone had some tradeoffs. On the upside, I didn't have to spend minutes or hours or days negotiating what time to get up. Negotiating whether to leave a stupid tourist attraction (Colonial Williamsburg and Disney World, I'm talking to you). Negotiating whether a sub-zero star room was worth the risk. Negotiating where to eat dinner, for crissakes. It was all about me!

Traveling alone made me more accessible to other people…yes, some weirdos, but also others who would not approach a person apparently occupied with a companion.

But some days were hard. I just saw some of the greatest artwork in the history of mankind, and I could only tell my journal. I just ate a horrible and disgusting meal, and I could only commiserate to my journal. I just had a blast at a baseball game, and I want to chant with someone, "[Insert-name-of-opposing team] sucks!" But yep, my journal. I guess my journal became my travel companion. At least I didn't have to negotiate with it; it couldn't talk. It could only listen. Go journal!

Whine, whine, whine.

Granted, sometimes I did phone my family (remember, pre-internet dark ages), but that was a crapshoot. Occasionally, they were excited for me, but it was equally likely they would tell me to get my sorry butt home.

Lesson learned: Loneliness is temporary and tolerable. If I was experiencing encounters that remained with me for the rest of my life, did it really matter if my journal was my only friend? No, ultimately it didn't.

Are We Done Yet?

When I still had three weeks remaining in Europe, I started whining to my journal. Of course, it had to listen.

I had reached the point of extreme cynicism and extreme fatigue. While in West Germany, I took a day trip to Trier, saw the postcard racks and gift shops that greeted me, and fled in horror. Another day trip to Rothenburg; it was so gosh-darn cute that I had to refrain from puking. Who writes these guidebooks? Obviously, not jaded people like me.

At some level, I felt guilty. Heck, some people work multiple jobs to keep a roof over their heads and food on the table. But poor me...I had just enough money in my pocket, an unlimited train pass, and Europe as my proverbial oyster. Of course part of me was gloating. "Bahaha, I'm here and you're not! You're working and I'm not!"

Whine, whine, whine.

Lesson learned (again): The lame destinations just kill time. And if I was whining about being footloose and free? I probably just needed a good night's sleep.

On the Road Again is Way Too Cliché, But I'll Go With It

One trip was winding down and I spent four days on a long, long coast-to-coast bus ride. It was fun in a weird way...or perhaps weird in a fun way.

Days 1 and 2 were just a blur. OMG, eating meals at numerous Bosselman's truck stops was an ordeal. Powdered-but-reconstituted eggs, days-old chicken...what the actual heck? On the upside, the Bosselman family had no need to worry about the overwhelming publicity resulting from being awarded a Michelin star.

At this point, I continued being a badass woman who was ready to tell any man to STFU if he violated my space. I had become fearless and just wanted men to leave me alone. For example:

- Elbowing a man who attempted to grope me when the bus rounded a bend.

- Shouting at a man who leered at me in a Cleveland bus station at 3 AM: "Stop staring at me! You're really pissing me off!"

195

- Responding to a pair on a bus leaving New York City, who had obviously just robbed a business, asking whether they frightened me. My response: "No, I am too broke for you to bother robbing me."

But this memory still cracks me up because I was tired, sore, and in need of a shower.

We were coasting into Bumtruck, Wyoming, at sunrise. The bus passed a skating rink named...wait for it...Roller City. Some guy on the bus was asking where we were. My response: "Roller City, Wyoming." And he believed me.

Lesson learned: Amazing what people would believe if I delivered it in an authoritative tone of voice. But it was sunrise; we all needed our coffee. And I needed to crack myself up.

Strangered in the Night

By Day 3, I was starting to get so antsy that I couldn't stand it. One of our stops was at a casino in Wendover, Nevada, and another stop in Wells, which was basically a lone bus station in the middle of nowhere. A lengthier stop was at an Elko casino. Played one hand at the table, and of course the dealer pulled an immediate blackjack. It was not my day.

We arrived in Reno for a rest stop for the driver, not us. We just wanted to be done. Such a long trip that I and my fellow passengers started getting delirious. As we continued the last leg of our trip to San Francisco, why not sing a song? Given the era, it was probably "Freebird." Let the jokes begin.

By Day 4, the bus was getting crazy. About seven people, three of whom were long-haulers like me. Being on a bus this long is really a unique experience, no less than the rest of my incredible journey. Now I was settled in with Cheryl (Philadelphia) and George (Tennessee) and I just knew we were going to make it. Surely the Greyhound driver knew how to navigate the mountain highway in the middle of the night. Thankfully, it was not snowstorm season.

When we finally arrived, we were dropped off in a horrible neighborhood. I didn't scare easy, but this was an exception. I had no idea the San Francisco Greyhound station was located in the pit of hell.

But then an angel named Bob descended upon me. He took me under his wing and invited me to hang out with him at Carl's Jr. Completely G-rated.

Bob was a professional gambler. Because our bus route included one of only two states with legalized gambling at the time, it made sense that a gambler was on board. I was initially puzzled; if he was a professional gambler, couldn't he afford better transportation than a rather smelly Greyhound bus? On the other hand, I didn't say he was a successful professional gambler.

We were gabbing while surrounded by several patrons with leaves and branches in their hair due to their unhoused status, along with a random middle-aged woman who was dressed rather well...who let her in? But who let me in? I didn't have branches in my hair, but I probably stunk after four days on a bus. Sorry.

I continued to be amazed by the sweet person who assured my safety until the sun came up. Even though Bob obviously had a somewhat checkered past, his assurances provided the perfect end to my first trip. Quotes:

- "Even living on the streets can be educational."

- "It's a special quality that you can find adventure in any situation."

- "You don't have to, and should not, lose the little kid in you."

It was such a great encounter. I even gave Bob one of my hoop earrings as a memento of our hours gabbing. It wasn't worth anything; it was the principle. Wouldn't that be a heartwarming ending to a movie? Let me know if you watch one with a comparable closing scene. "Breakfast Club," anyone? Even though the movie was released in February 1985, I promise I hadn't seen it. Heck, I still haven't seen it from start to finish.

Lesson learned: Don't be afraid of people...well okay, some of them. However, I am still grateful that I was a twentysomething young woman traveling alone, but was only genuinely afraid three times. My angels appeared when I needed them, and I certainly needed one that night.

Learning to Fly After I Sleep On a Floor

Time to fly back across the pond, departing from the Frankfurt airport. I had everything I needed: backpack, passport, a few German marks, a few American dollars for when I arrived.

My flight was leaving at 6:30 AM. I didn't trust myself to board the Frankfurt U-Bahn at 4:00 AM, constantly crossing my fingers that I wouldn't miss my flight. I decided to spend the night in the airport terminal, which was open 24-7.

Because I had spent the night in an airport a couple of times, it didn't frighten me. The easy drill:

1. Check in. Duh. Move on through airport security to the safety of a terminal rather than a random train station or bus bench.

2. Find a suitable place to sleep. The seats had the strategically placed armrests that would make sleeping pretty uncomfortable. Okay, let's go with the carpeted floor. I could safely stash my backpack in a locker, even though it would cost money. My cushy down jacket would be my pillow.

3. Go to sleep, which didn't take long because I was exhausted. I'd have been willing to gab with similarly impoverished travelers, but there were none.

4. Sleep until the early morning airport terminal activity woke me up, then groggily grab some coffee before I board my flight.

5. After I was seated, invoke my usual trick to claim a row for my own. I coughed up a lung until everyone chose their seats to ensure I wouldn't pass on my theoretical virus. In all fairness, I'm not sure I had to do that on this particular flight. But I have done that when warranted, and it especially amuses our daughter. (Perhaps I should not share this tip. Because it works so well, I may be faced with a plane full of people fake-coughing the next time I fly Southwest.)

6. Go back to sleep, pleased that I didn't waste money on a room. In all honesty, the terminal was more comfortable than some of my zero-star hotels…the restrooms were clean

and I knew there were no armed criminals in my midst. Shoutout to airport security.

Lesson learned: Sometimes, seemingly scary experiences are not at all scary. It was much nicer to sleep at the airport than to try to schlep myself out of bed at 4 AM. Cheaper, too.

American Girl, Complete With English Speakers

Flew into Philadelphia from Frankfurt. As usual, I had no advance reservation, was sooo tired, but had to find a place to sleep. Rooms were expensive and I was almost out of money.

I had to stay in a zero-star—make that a sub-zero star—hovel, but I didn't care. It was probably the worst dump I ever stayed in; the clerk was behind bulletproof glass. (Unfortunately, I stayed in another hovel of this nature at age 51. I never learn.) The towels in my room were horrible, and a hall bath run? Maybe. Perhaps I could just hold it.

I think I chose to use the hall bath while incorporating my badass walk and making sure I locked my door behind me. A shower? Are you kidding me? The theoretical bath towel was the size of a kitchen towel. And only God knows when it had last been laundered.

But American TV in actual English was great. "Golden Girls!" "Cheers!" Bring them on!

I loved Europe, but was happy to be back in our great nation. I could speak English and not have to resort to gesturing in a valiant attempt to communicate. I could look forward to eating an American breakfast in the morning without cultural guilt, even including scrapple. A Philly thing…not nearly as disgusting as it may seem.

Lesson learned: Bulletproof glass is a warning sign, but I didn't die. Maybe it was a sign that I was safer.

Greatest Quote Ever

My final trip was coming to an end.

Was I ready to go home? Exactly where was home? I kinda-sorta missed my family, but could they appreciate the epiphany I experienced during my travels? Could they stop worrying? Could they appreciate that I had not, after all, ended up in a ditch? Could they accept that I had a great and amazing experience…on my own? And could I accept that I was destined to go back to the workaday world rather than write great and bemused prose?

Ultimately, I went back to that world because income is good, but at least I'm hopefully writing great and bemused prose now. Better late than never.

For the second year in a row, last stop was Philadelphia before heading back to the left coast and reality. I managed to stay in a very comfy hotel. It was a splurge, but that's what credit cards are for. I felt naughty. And I expected to earn income in the next couple of weeks, so what the heck.

I struck up a conversation with one of the employees. I told her of some of my adventures. Her admiring response: "You've been basically fucking around for most of the last two years?" Yep, I had been. And yes, the potty mouth is necessary to quote her in its entirety. I promise, I threw a dollar in the swear jar.

Lesson not learned: I should have taken the time to get to know her. She was impressed with me in a very sweet manner, and I wish I could remember her name.

Time to Move On

I have loved being your raconteur, regaling you with my stories of when I was a twentysomething. Who knew WTF will happen on any random day? Nonstop adventures. And I learned so many lessons!

But what happens when you realize those days are mostly in the past?

I don't intend to start an "organ recital" (thanks, brother-in-law—I guess—for that term). But it is an odd realization that I may not see much more of the world, even though I've seen more than your average bear. That would be Yogi, the cartoon resident of Jellystone Park. Another question for your elders?

Yes, I am subjected to the gosh-darn prescription drug ads during my old-person TV shows. And no, I don't need any of those drugs that will cure you if they don't kill you…so far, anyway. I guess I need to watch more channels targeted to younger people. Or cut the cord, for crissakes. But is Jeopardy really an old-person show? I mean, come on. Current contestants know more about Netflix than I do. And TikTok. And hip-hop.

In all honesty, though, I hate three things:

- That I probably can no longer cope with the trips I took many years ago...too many stairs. The Eiffel Tower? Leaning Tower of Pisa? Statue of Liberty? Bahaha! Some days in this season of my life, I avoid the 14 stairs to the second level of our house. Stinks, but I am probably being a drama queen.

- That I never did the 500-mile Camino de Santiago. However, I doubt I could have coped with it even as a twentysomething. Kudos to everyone who has done it, although it sounds hot, exhausting, and brutal. But aside from that, a wonderful journey. If you are intrigued, read "Walking With Sam" by Andrew McCarthy. Greatest. Memoir. Ever. I actually finished it.

- That I am actually okay with not seeing any more of the world. What became of the wanderlust woman who was always up for a frugal trip? Oh yeah, perhaps she has subscribed to the notion that "if you want the comforts of home, you should stay there." I heart my home, my husband, and my small town.

In dubious fairness to me, I have never been interested in Asian countries. And India, with the 100 required vaccinations to avoid the risk of a tragic and rapid death? I don't think so. Japanese and Chinese art is just dumb. Sorry; please don't judge me. I know I can be ignorant.

I would love to see more of South America--especially Uruguay and the Galapagos Islands--but it takes sooo long to get there.

Frankly, I would still love to see Amsterdam, as well as to experience London with my husband. In order to fly across the pond, though, I need first class. Because of our credit card frequent flyer miles, it's doable. But please don't ask me to fly coach on an umpteen-hour flight.

At this point in my travels, I want a journey that lets me sleep, eat reasonably good food, and privately gloat until I groggily arrive at my destination. I have only flown first class once, but it was so, so, so amazing. And because I was wearing a Tom Petty T-shirt, a member of the flight crew actually thought I worked for him. I was too honest to pretend I did, but he persisted in his suspicion, and asked my kids, seated a few rows back, if I was being coy and/or modest. I love hypothetical bragging rights, but I did not misrepresent myself. I promise.

If you are still in reasonably good shape, coach is tolerable, but not on United Airlines. Their seats are tiny, and I only weigh 115 pounds; my husband was probably miserable. But on a seriously long flight, I needs me my first class. Again, readers, I am not a wealthy person. But OMG, I know how to work the credit card rewards.

I hope my readers will be inspired to find their own adventures in our beautiful world. I especially want to encourage my proverbial sisters to venture out. You don't need a guy to be your bodyguard; just work on your badass walk. I don't need to provide a YouTube link as to what that entails; you be you.

Shoutout to my younger readers. After you marry and have adorable babies who have the habit of routinely puking and pooping at the most inopportune times, you can remember when you were footloose and fancy-free. Trust me, it will get you through the challenging times. It got me through them.

Lesson imparted: Go see the world! I'm looking forward to reading your memoirs. Thanks for reading mine.

About the Author

Toni Jeffrey is a writer living in California's beautiful Santa Cruz Mountains. She wishes she had the guts to dye her hair purple.